POSITIVE HABITS GET RESULTS

FOCUS ON SUCCESS, FIND YOUR PURPOSE

DONNA PORTLAND

BALBOA.PRESS

A DIVISION OF HAY HOUSE

Balboa Press books may be ordered through booksellers or by contacting:

Balboa Press
A Division of Hay House
1663 Liberty Drive
Bloomington, IN 47403
www.balboapress.com.au
AU TFN: 1 800 844 925 (Toll Free inside Australia)
AU Local: 0283 107 086 (+61 2 8310 7086 from outside Australia)

ISBN: 978-1-5043-2257-7 (sc)
ISBN: 978-1-5043-2280-5 (e)

Print information available on the last page.

Balboa Press rev. date: 10/28/2020

DEDICATION

This book is dedicated to all who truly want to move forward and get the most from life.

It will take courage and a committed decision.

I hope that my story and research help you to get your life on track.

EPIGRAPH

**"Depending on what they are, our habits
will either make us or break us.
We become what we repeatedly do". [1]**

Sean Covey, Author.

[1] Quoted from "The 7 Habits Of Highly Effective Teens".

CONTENTS

FOREWORD

by Sharon Cullington, Parenting Coach and Expert, Author of "Excuse me: Who Put The Kids In Charge?"

Some years ago, I met Donna Portland at a book publishing event. It was a packed room yet somehow we gravitated towards each other, like fireflies to a light. It turned out that we shared a lot in common: sense of humour, sense of fun, positivity, motherhood, sisterhood, authorship, coaching, and most of all a dream to make a difference in the world.

After hearing each other's stories, it was apparent that we also had in common an attitude toward life that left no room for complaining about the past. We were busy growing and moving forward and we both wanted to take people with us on that journey.

I was struck not only by Donna's honestly and authenticity, but I also loved how she openly admitted that most of her life's challenges were due to her choices and I noticed how she was not making any excuses. She also freely shared with me and anyone who asked, exactly what it takes to turn your life around.

Donna's endless courage and determination inspired me to try harder, to be better as well. Finding the energy to keep going forward can sometimes be the toughest challenge, yet Donna has some tricks up her sleeve that I have never seen or heard before. In 'Positive Habits Get Results' it's all revealed and explained in ways that are simple to follow and fun to use.

If you've made a decision and commitment to become the best version of yourself too you will find out exactly how to do that by following the step by step process that she has devised that takes you from your thoughts and hopes to realizing your dreams.

Donna is just an ordinary person, from an ordinary background, yet she has managed to achieve extraordinary results by following the process herself. She has attained something that so many fail to achieve: a sense of her true self and true purpose, which she lives authentically each day. She has transformed from being an unhappy unfulfilled woman, to being wonderfully engaging, generous and truly inspirational.

Her intention in writing this book is to serve and inspire as many people as possible and I know that your life will change even as you move through the book.

I wish you well on your journey through life and on getting the results you seek, and I know that this book will help you.

Namaste, Sharon

ABOUT THE AUTHOR

Donna Portland currently lives in Sydney Australia. She will be living there until at least after her son finishes school. In early 2024, she will fulfil the dream she has had for the last ten years of so, of travelling to her favourite country – Italy – and renting a large villa somewhere for six months … a year … maybe two …!

The plan is to reside there whilst her son spends his gap year (or two …) working on superyachts in Europe. (Well that is what he says he wants to do! and Donna is hoping that he sticks to the plan.) During that time Donna plans to become an Italian: speak the language, live like a local, cook and eat the food, drink the wine, live the life and explore her creative endeavours of drawing, painting and writing. Donna is already planning the steps she needs to take! It is a dream that she will turn into a reality.

Donna is a Master NLP coach and hypnotherapist and works as a Success Coach, helping people reach their aspirations and dreams to achieve their success - whatever that means to them.

Donna had an 'awakening' some years ago and began a fabulous journey towards finding meaning in her life. She managed to get clear on the strategies she needed to adopt to reach her goals and take her life to the next level.

Studying NLP and hypnotherapy, gave more practical application to the psychology that Donna had studied at university many years previously, and the NLP techniques get faster results.

Donna gets joy and fulfilment from helping others move forward positively in their lives.

Open your eyes and your heart.
Life is a precious gift.

You have freedom.
 You have choice.

Use your time wisely:
 Strive to make the most of it.

Fill it with love,
 joy, peace and appreciation.

Donna Portland

PREFACE

Some background on how I came to write this book:

Born to middle class parents in the 60's I started life in the 'burbs' of Sydney, Australia. The three sisters in my family attended a proper private girls' school initially and we lived the typical family life until my father left when I was ten. I did not see him again for some 23 years, but that is another story.

We moved to a rented house in Surry Hills, an inner-city suburb of Sydney. Life as we knew it had changed significantly. It was quite a culture shock and money was scarce. My mother had to go back to work after 16 years of being a housewife. Life was 'no frills' but we got by. Mum did a spectacular job of providing love and care. My siblings and I quickly learned to pitch in to help and also to do for ourselves.

As a shy teenager with low self-confidence, I found socialising uncomfortable. I did not have the emotional skills to match my high IQ evidenced by my academic results. After leaving school, as an adult governing my own life, I discovered some self-confidence in my abilities as a nurse and invested myself into the profession. The job was rewarding and enjoyable and I loved working hard.

After a year as a registered nurse I left that career for several reasons, the chief of which was my boundless curiosity to experience a great many things in life. Another reason was to get away from 'institutionalised' personalities.

I wanted to travel and see what else was out there in the world.

All my life I had heard my parent's and various other influencers' voices in my ear saying **"study hard, get a good job, put your head down and work hard, get married, buy a house, have a family and live happily ever after".** As you know, society generally advocates this prescription to everyone.

Following the advice, I had many interesting jobs during my working life, the most unusual of which was working in the professional yachting industry in the European and USA waters for over six years.

I met a man and after four years working together with him on yachts we got married, and two years later we became land-based in Sydney because it was time for a change, I was approaching my late thirties and we wanted to start a family. It took quite some time, but we eventually had a wonderful son, who continues to be a source of joy.

My problem was that, in all other aspects of my life, I just could not achieve the 'happily ever after' part.

Fast forward twenty years and I was living a flat-chat, crazy-busy life as a mother, wife, and business owner (of a recruitment company) working fulltime at *all* of my occupations (as mother, wife, house manager, business owner) until November 2017.

Exhausted and unmotivated was how I always seemed to feel. The truth, that I came to understand, was that I was living 'unconsciously' most of the time - just going through the motions of daily life - relieved to get to the end of each day and would then collapse into a chair in front of the TV.

Looking back now, I realise that we live in a society that promotes constant comparison of ourselves to others. This was me too. I had succumbed. We are bombarded with marketing from all sources that tells us we need this and that to measure up, that we are not enough unless we wear X, drive Y and holiday at Z, etc. etc. You are aware of this of course! We are influenced into buying far too many clothes, purchasing cars or holidays that we cannot really afford, having plastic surgery that we don't really need, and the list of influence goes on. The main problem here is that all those 'things' that we were convinced we needed - to be happy or fulfilled or whatever we were chasing - just don't deliver. We get those things and there is still a hole.... So, we go and buy more! The cycle never ends, and we are never fully satisfied.

The other thing we humans do is constantly assign meaning to the things that happen. We immerse ourselves in the story we have told ourselves about what happened, and we become unhappily stuck in that story!

Humans also tend to always complain about things - aloud as well as inwardly! Come on, be honest: I challenge you to monitor your current set of complaints as they occur to you every day! Write them down - become aware - and watch how your list grows!! This mode of being is commonplace and is the norm in our lives. We become comfortably numb about this over time. We barely notice what a robotic life we are living.... until we wake up – *if* we wake up!

Over the years I had grown further and further apart from my partner. Rather than face that reality and do something about it, I squashed that realisation down as it seemed unsolvable. Instead I devoted most of my time to caring for my son and managing his life, whilst juggling the household workload with a demanding business. On the outside it appeared as though

I had it all: a husband and child, lived in a large and lovely home, drove a prestige car, had my own business and all the material comforts. However, life held little satisfaction - I felt unloved, lonely, and disconnected and was deeply unhappy.

I have learned that disconnection between partners in a relationship, especially after many years together, is common! Couples often say that the attraction they had once felt towards their partner just faded away over time. In many cases when this happens people either go into a form of denial and they focus attention elsewhere in their lives where they *can* find some joy, and many retreat into their work/career. This does not bode well for the growth or continuation of a relationship...

In my life for many years I felt lonely and empty. Over time I grew resentful and felt helpless. I was fearful about the future and felt stressed and stuck - working crazy hours to try to distract myself from loneliness and have something to focus on. I also wanted to feel that I had some kind of purpose. However, my personal 'tank' was empty. I gave no time for myself. After working all day, I'd come home and cook dinner, clean up afterwards, check my son's homework and re-check my emails, put my son to bed, tidy up the rest of the house, do some washing and ironing, and would often put in a few more hours of work on the computer (for my recruitment business).

After years of this I was so worn out that I literally had nothing left to give. Every night after shutting down my computer, I would sit mindlessly in front of the TV for hours on end. My brain had gone to mush and it became the habit to drink way too much red wine to numb myself against my misery and loneliness. Sounds like a form of depression doesn't it?

How do you find the courage to change things? Hard for me to do because I felt so bad about myself. I felt worthless having gained over 20-kg (45 pounds) of extra weight — no wonder with the amount of wine, paté and chocolate that I consumed every night! I was miserable and unable to find the motivation I needed to help myself ...

I had gone into denial about many aspects of my life: my weight, the state of my marriage, and that I had allowed myself to sink into depression. I felt closed, separate, and unable to communicate. For years I did not feel any personal connection. Communication had been slowly starved out over many years. Life felt like mindless clocking on and clocking off each day. At the time it seemed easier to deny - to avoid taking action, but I hated myself for my inaction.

Then something happened in October 2017 that spoke volumes to me - the death of a friend at the age of 49. It was not the first time I had experienced a death. When I discovered that he was not living his life the way he wanted to - that he felt totally stuck - it spoke a loud and clear message to me. I too was NOT living the way I wanted to! This sad event was the catalyst I needed to finally wake up and take a good hard look at my own life and its trajectory.

The ducks had finally lined up and I fessed up *to myself* (and others) that I was *not* happy and had been wasting away - for years. The only sane way forward was to cut my losses and set about reinventing my life. So, in my fifties I made the inevitable decision, that took a huge dose of courage: I stepped up and left my old life. It was not an easy journey. There are so many life-changes that you go through when you leave a long-term relationship and way of life (well over twenty years in my case). It is hard to imagine the emotional ups and downs that you will inevitably go through. I just knew with conviction that I had to face my fears and do it anyway in order to find joy again. My pain was too great to leave things as they were. There was a feeling inside me that knew things had to change because I had so much more life to live!

So began my mission: I embarked on a journey that has transformed my life in the most satisfying and positive ways, learning to connect to my 'higher self'. I did this by lots of personal searching and enquiry, and also with the help of a coach. I broke through the constraints and fears of the ego and I discovered my inner strength and confidence.

My first step was to commit to myself (*and* my coach) and do the work of course, and the results are richly evident. I focussed on my outcome which was to reinvent my life anew, follow my passions and discover who *I* am on my own. My aim was to re-discover Donna Portland. She used to be a smiling, fun and lively gal who was always out there doing things, meeting people, and discovering fascinating things about life, being joyful in the process.

These days without any prompting people tell me often how much I have changed! I know that it's because my energy is different. Now I am unafraid to be me. I have let go of feeling judged, let go of comparisons, and constant complaints, and I am focussed on gratitude. People comment on how much brighter, happier, and present I am. It is great to hear it of course - but primarily it's great to feel it!

My second step towards reinventing my life anew was to I move out of the house that I had lived in for the last ten years and re-establish myself independently.

Straight away I tried the online dating apps and websites because I really needed a social life and some company! I needed to rediscover who I was. So, I started going out and meeting new people. Some of that can be fun, but the difficult part about socialising is being brave enough to step out alone. A lot of people you knew as a couple just leave you out - they don't know what to say, so I guess it's easier for them to keep away … That is pretty disappointing, as I would have welcomed some moral support. I suppose they feel awkward inviting a single when everyone else is coupled up?

The results of my foray were that I made some interesting friends and went out and had some fun and distraction, but I was not finding many kindred souls – the kind I could couple up with. I think that the lesson there was that I needed to first find my own inner joy in order to bring that to another relationship. Being able to see the gift in your experiences is such an important thing. Attracting the right kind of person is paramount to being able to form a good relationship!

My journey of self-discovery began with regaining my lost energy and this was the primary mission! There was a lot of work to do and I needed to maintain motivation and focus.

My brain was way too busy, so my coach helped me find a meditation practice that worked. The benefits are far more than I thought were possible. I have conquered the random and negative thinking patterns and most importantly, removed limiting beliefs and blocked energies. I have taken responsibility for my life choices and made a decision to leave the past in the past and move forward with purpose!

After six weeks with my coach I felt I had truly 'woken up'.

I carried on studying and reading things to help me continue to heal and grow.

I attended art classes as I enjoy painting and drawing and wanted to tap into the treasure trove of my creativity and self-expression.

I reverted to my maiden name; I needed to be one hundred percent me.

I read a lot, plus attended seminars, and talks on self-development and the like.

My aim was (and is) to grow as a person and rebuild my life and embark on a physical and spiritual journey to find my happiness from within.

But, LIFE GETS IN THE WAY ...

To be honest, some of the time I would take two steps forward, then a step back. Things would be going well and then I would have a set-back that I found hard to deal with. I would plunge back into gloom and stress and the result was that I was nowhere near where I wanted to be. So, I went back for more coaching.

I will admit that I had always been a bit sceptical about 'alternative' therapies and ideas. I had shied away from anything that wasn't conservative and aligned with western medicine. Over the course of my life though, my personal experience has revealed that conventional attitudes and ways of living life just weren't working - not for me and not for many people.

I am not discarding the appropriate uses for doctors and health care professionals, but I have realised that if you are searching and you truly want to learn then the teacher appears!

That is a paraphrased quote from Buddha! Jesus Christ also said a similar thing about finding what you truly seek! That *is* exactly what happens when you start looking for your answers.

More coaching: what did I have to lose? I wanted to completely lose the emotional pain and the useless thinking that wasted so much of my time! I wanted to continue gaining self-belief and self-confidence. My search for my understanding and peace has been so rewarding.

It is usual for people to use coaches for physical health and a fitness regime. I committed to exercising every day! Usually I would walk (fast and up hills to get the heartrate up) but I also started doing other forms of exercise to keep it interesting and to build muscle. Unlike previously, my diet is now 'mindful' and a firm part of my daily life.

The most amazing transformation has taken place. The needle on the scales had just kept going up and up for the last ten years until I changed my mindset and experienced a huge energy shift. I saw my weight start to drop and keep dropping! It has now stabilised on my perfect height-to-weight ratio. These days it is quite obvious to those who have known me for some years that I've lost over 20kgs (45 pounds) and have way more energy and zest, a big smile on my face and a sparkle in my eye! I then found that I had the most wonderful first world problem of having to either get my clothes taken in at the dressmakers or to give them away and buy new ones!

So due to the new habits that I have embraced, I have been able to learn and grow and have increased my physical and mental strength. I feel an enormous amount of gratitude to learn that life was not just happening *to* me, but that there were lessons - gifts - along the way in my journey! I just needed to wake up, make a decision and a commitment to myself to regain my energy and claim back my power.

I had (and still have) so many goals, and so far have achieved so much that it astounds me! Mostly it is inner change: a sense of connection to the world, confidence, peace, and self-love. These days, I am finding that this change has had the effect that I am regularly meeting wonderful people and strengthening my relationships generally. The attitude is to just have fun and enjoying meeting people. With this new mindset along with self-love and healing, I am organically finding compatible people who enhance my social experience. I am not *trying* to find "the one" or the "soul mate", or "someone to complete me" as so many people state on their dating profiles. That is putting a very large and unrealistic expectation onto anyone that you meet. I realised that the feeling of wholeness and a complete life and inner happiness comes from within each one of us. You need to achieve the state of happiness and completion by yourself, and then you will have something to bring to a relationship!

◊ ◊ ◊ ◊ ◊

I own a recruitment agency in a very niche sector (yacht crew, jet crew and private/domestic staff – butlers, housekeepers, chefs, nannies, etc.) It is called Elite Private Staff, and I am assisted by wonderful colleagues who are positively minded, knowledgeable, talented, and devoted. Whilst they have shouldered the workload I have had the opportunity to document my journey back to vitality and prime health, as well as to find my life purpose. I have had the opportunity to study to extend my communications skillset to include Neurolinguistic Programming (NLP) coaching and hypnotherapy. I have done this because I have gotten so much out of coaching that I wanted to also help others achieve the same breakthroughs as I have.

I now offer coaching to those who want to go forward and take their life to the next level! The powerful NLP coaching tools that I have learned help people transform their lives. If you truly want to move forward and get the most from your life, all it takes is a committed decision to act now.

I feel blessed and privileged to do what I do and work with the people I do, as well as having friends that make my life richer. Every day is an opportunity for growth and expansion, so I focus on making every moment count.

It is true that we live only a short time on the planet, and we owe it to ourselves and our families to do the best job we can in living it well.

I hope that you can join me on the journey and create your future. This book aims to share with you my discovery and compilation of knowledge to assist you to get where you want to go so that you can move forward positively to live life on your own terms.

My gift to you is this book – my first. All these steps have been so worthwhile to me to help me to progress. My hope is that it is the same for you.

With love, Donna

INTRODUCTION

"When a flower doesn't bloom
You fix the environment
in which it grows,
not the flower."

Alexander Den Heijer

The book is about progressing your life.

It is about making positive changes that last.

Know that, as a person, you are fine as you are. Perhaps the environment you have created in your life needs to change though. Maybe then the flower will grow!

Perhaps you have slipped into a habit of living unconsciously - living like you are on autopilot – just making it to the end of the day ...?

Perhaps your daily habits have contributed to an unsatisfactory life for you?

Are you lacking motivation, or is there something holding you back from reaching your goals?

Think about this idea: *If you're not growing, you are dying. When you stagnate, you wilt.*

Various learned souls have been quoted saying much the same. American writer and visual artist William S Burroughs said: **"When you stop growing you start dying."**

Steve Siebold[2] said: **"You're either growing or dying. Stagnation does not exist in the universe?"**

Dustin W Stout[3] said: **"Grow or Die. There's no such thing as stagnant. Being stagnant is a lie that keeps you comfortable with not growing."**

The popular modern-day practical psychologist and educator Anthony Robbins[4] teaches:

Progress = Happiness!

I wholeheartedly agree. To quote him directly: *"If you want to have ongoing joy and fulfillment in your life, the secret is just one word - progress."*

It is an idea that many coaches and teachers talk about. I read a particularly insightful blog written by psychologist Vanessa Rose who said:

> *"Despite what many of us think (and hope), there is no one level of success that will grant us permission to coast through the rest of our lives without a care in the world. Often, we hang our hopes of a simple and fantastic future on that one goal we aim to achieve. But even when we achieve it and revel in that sweet victory, we still eventually find ourselves back in the same headspace as before. Why? Because* **achievement is temporary**, *and* **our goals move**. *You know what doesn't move?* **Progress**. *That's why it's been said that progress equals happiness."* [5]

Her blog is well worth the complete read. The idea is that by focussing on achievement rather than progress, we put pressure on the wrong actions and outcomes. By focussing on progress, we are granted larger feelings of success. Obviously not everyone has the same abilities. We each are on our own journey, so progress is individual.

2   https://stevesiebold.net/
3   https://dustinstout.com/
4   https://www.tonyrobbins.com/
5   https://yesgurus.com/blog/progress-equals-happiness/

Do you agree? Have you stopped to imagine what ongoing progress actually looks like for you? What it feels like?

Have you asked yourself "What is fulfillment (to me)?"

"What would need to happen to make me feel fulfilled?"

Start a little journal for yourself now. Pull out your pen and paper and makes some notes whilst you read. I am sure that you will be filling your book with highly useful ideas and insights!

Congratulations if you are already there and feel totally joyful and fulfilled! I would love to talk to you and spend some time. You are the kind of person that I want to associate with - often! But I suspect that you do not always feel this way. That's why you are reading this book. That's OK of course. We are all on a journey and it is an uncommon thing to find people who don't have some issues from time to time or who, like me, had started life okay but then things went askew, and I lost my juice.

There are myriad things that get in the way of enjoying life. There are so many distractions. We have responsibilities: caring for children, partner and family, work obligations, debt, complicated relationships, disease, disability, divorce ... that take up our time and our headspace. We use these complaints and excuses for not doing the things we have said we wanted to do or achieve!

The best question to ask is **"What can I do to start along the path to progress and move toward happiness _now_?"**

The thing that worked for me was to create a new set of rituals that started me on the path of progress. Once you start down that path, and invest yourself in this pursuit, you are certain to find the joy you desire and deserve.

I created a Daily Habit list.

I have read extensively and made a compendium of thoughts about ways you can make some changes to your behaviours (to your daily habits) that would have a lasting and positive impact over time and enable you to reach your goals.

Why do our daily habits matter? In his quote John Dryden (1631, English poet and literary critic) makes it clear:

"We first make our habits, and then our habits make us."

Think awhile about the truth of this statement. It is the things that we consistently do, day in and day out, that govern the successful achievement of our goal(s). The athlete will train for many many hours. The musician will practise her instrument. The actor will rehearse his lines over and over again. The ballerina will train and practise her dance moves repeatedly. These people reach expertise because they trained their bodies and their minds.

You can do it too! It might not be running or hurdling, dancing or playing an instrument, but it will be gaining control over your mind, practising discipline and single-mindedness towards the pursuits that are meaningful to you.

There are 18 chapters in this book. The first seven deal with aspects of your physicality. The following eleven concern your headspace. As you read, you will intuitively choose to read the chapters that are the most meaningful to you and to start incorporating some of these ideas into your daily life - with positive result.

My recommendation would be to start with adopting three to five new habits: the ones that you need now! Then as you manage to naturally incorporate them into your daily life, it will be easy to re-read through the list and choose to adopt some more.

Know that after a while it won't be a burden to "have to do" these things because you will either become addicted to how good you feel or how healthy you've become that it just feels right and becomes second nature.

I made a list of my top ten habits to adopt and stuck it up on my wall where I would see it every day. If you like, like me, you can tick things off the list. It won't take long before you feel enormous change.

PART 1

CHAPTER 1

SLEEP & WAKING

It is common amongst human beings that when you are in stress or a low point in your life you have difficulty sleeping - getting off to sleep or getting quality sleep. We have all experienced this.

After I had made the decision to turn my life around, at times my mind was in overwhelm and sometimes my thoughts ran in circles and I could not shut them off. Chaotic thought patterns were causing me anxiety and stress.

Everyone has experienced times like this when important issues crop up in your life and dominate your thoughts. It can become a big issue if it causes sleep disturbance and your cumulative lack of sleep makes matters worse and further depletes your reserves. There is a knock-on effect into other areas of your life if you don't get it under control - and soon!

The importance of sleep

Sleep plays a vital role in maintaining good health and well-being in your life. To help protect your mental health, physical health, quality of life, and safety you need to get sufficient quality sleep at the right times. You spend about one-third of your life doing it and it's as essential to survival as food and water. Without sleep you cannot form or maintain the pathways in your brain that let you learn and create new memories, and it is harder to concentrate and respond quickly. In children and teenagers, sleep also helps support growth and development.

During sleep, your body is working to maintain your physical health and support healthy brain function. Your brain and body stay remarkably active while you sleep. Research suggests that sleep plays a housekeeping role that removes toxins in your brain that build up while you are awake. Sleep affects almost every type of tissue and system in the body: the brain, heart, and lungs, metabolism, immune function, mood, and disease resistance. Ongoing sleep deficiency or getting poor quality sleep can raise your risk for some chronic health problems such as high blood pressure, cardiovascular disease, diabetes, depression, and obesity. It also can affect how well you think, react, work, learn, and get along with others.

How much sleep is enough?

The amount of sleep you need each day will change over the course of your life and sleep needs do vary from person to person. There is no magic number of hours for sleep that works for everybody of the same age. According to the American Academy of Sleep Medicine (AASM[6]) **Teenagers from 13-18 years are recommended to get from 8-10 hours of sleep per day. Adults (over 18 years) are recommended 7–9 hours of sleep per day.** It is common after age 60, that night sleeps tend to be shorter, lighter, and interrupted for a variety of reasons. It is more likely that those who take medications will experience more sleep interference.

Sleep Deprivation

Generally, people are getting less sleep than they need, and this can often be due to longer work hours and the habit of indulging in round-the-clock entertainment and stimulants that they consume.

Are you in sleep debt? If you habitually lose sleep or choose to sleep less than you need, the sleep loss does add up. For example, if you lose one to two hours of sleep each night, you will have a sleep debt of 7 - 14 hours over the week. So, if you find that you sleep more on days off work then it could be a sure sign that you are not getting enough sleep, and this is why you need to 'catch up'. Doing this may also upset your body's rhythm for sleeping and waking.

Taking a nap may provide a short-term boost in alertness and performance but napping does not provide all of the other benefits of night-time sleep. So, you cannot really make up for lost sleep.

Some people may not realise that they are sleep deficient and may not be aware of the risks. It is well documented that truck drivers, with limited or poor-quality sleep, may still think that they can function well and be capable of driving, yet the statistics around trucking accidents and deaths are staggering!

Of course these are not the only people affected by sleep deficiency. It can affect everyone. There have been all sorts of industrial accidents, ships going aground and aeroplane crashes where fatigue and sleep deficiency has played a major part.

---

[6] https://aasm.org/

DONNA PORTLAND

Sleep deficiency has been linked with the increased risk of obesity in teenagers and other age groups and has also been linked to sadness, depression, suicide, risk-taking behaviour, problems paying attention, or lack of motivation, social problems including impulsiveness, stress, and mood swings!

Aim for better quality of sleep.

By ensuring that you receive enough good quality sleep each night, you may find that you are more productive during the day and feel much better and happier. You *can* take steps to improve your sleep habits.

1. **Spend time outdoors and be physically active during the day.**

2. **Keep a routine or schedule** as much as possible, as this will maintain a healthy sleep/ waking rhythm.

3. **Make sure that you allow yourself enough time to sleep**.

4. **Eat dinner earlier to avoid large meals close to bedtime**. *It is the same for drinking alcohol, nicotine, and caffeine (coffee, tea, cola, chocolate).*

5. **Go to bed earlier.** *Do you really need to watch more TV...? Did you know that the blue light from your TV screen or mobile phone suppresses the production of sleep hormone melatonin? The light signals the brain that it is time to be awake! There is plenty of research on this, so feel free to explore further – especially if you need to convince your kids that they need to reign in the night screen time.*

6. **Start winding down at least an hour before bedtime.** *Avoid exercise just before bedtime and instead use this quiet time to read. It is a great habit to increase your reading (as you will discover as you keep reading this book), so here is a wonderful opportunity to indulge this positive habit and assist your brain to get you ready for sleep.*

7. **Your bedroom: ensure that your bedroom is dark, cool and quiet.** *Avoid having a TV or computer in your room as those flashing lights and beeps will disturb you.*

8. **Evening meditations and/or relaxation techniques are a great idea before bedtime.**

9. **You may need to see a doctor* if your sleep issue does not respond to these suggestions.** **But first give it a few weeks for the changes to kick in.*

10. **Technology may help**

You can use a smart phone app, or a bedside monitor, and various wearable items (including bracelets, smart watches, and headbands) to collect data to analyse your sleep. These apps can record sounds and movement during your sleep and record the hours slept, whilst monitoring heartrate and respirations.

There are apps that play 'white noise' or produce light that stimulates melatonin production, and some use gentle vibrations to help you sleep and wake. I often used the white noise apps when I couldn't sleep. My favourites were rainforest, rain sounds, and beach noise. It works very well.

Wake up early

Starting the day well sets you up for a great day to follow. That way you will be organised for the day! Many successful people live by this maxim, *"If you win the morning, you win the day."*

"If you win the morning, you win the day".

Tim Ferris [7]

---

7   Take a look at this video: https://www.entrepreneur.com/video/288128 Author and entrepreneur Tim Ferriss explains his routine and why what he does is helpful.

Author and entrepreneur Tim Ferriss put forward this idea as he has a routine to set him up for success. I agree that this will work for many people, so it is worth trying it out for yourself.

Why wake early? Here are some reasons why it's a great idea:

1. **You will have time to eat a decent breakfast in peace,** rather than rushing out the door grabbing some 'convenient' substance posing as food - or skip the meal altogether and get by on coffee. Skipping breakfast is likely to lead to poor eating habits later in the day, i.e. donuts, high sugar "energy" bars, fast foods.

2. **Your skin will respond well to a restful night's sleep.** You will also have time to cleanse, exfoliate and moisturise adequately.

3. **You will have more time for exercise** (walking, gym, cycling, swimming, boxing, yoga... and so on) if you rise early. It is common for people to dip out on their afterwork exercise session because of other commitments at work or simply because they have just run out of energy. You know how that feels at the end of the day! So, if you get your exercise done early - it's done! This was the thing that was essential for my success in regaining my fitness. **GET IT DONE** – EVERY DAY.

4. **You will have better concentration and ability to focus.** If you can create time where you have peace and fewer interruptions, you will be able to increase your productivity whilst you're at your peak of alertness.

5. People who get up early are naturally sleepier when it is the normal time to go to bed each night. So, being on a predictable routine will help you sleep better each night and wake feeling more rested.

6. You may find that your daily commute is easier if you leave an hour earlier and beat all the traffic.

7. Early in the morning it is so peaceful and quiet. When there are zero distractions you can truly enjoy valuable 'me time'.

What is the best time to wake up?

It is always a personal choice and different for each individual, but most successful people will say 5am.

The medical community would generally agree on sunrise or 6:30am.

The goal would be to wake up after having at least seven good hours of restful sleep, after having gone to bed before 11pm.

How to get up? Here are some tips:

1. **Go to bed earlier than usual**. That way you will get enough hours of sleep, and you will not feel deprived when the alarm sounds. If you are not tired when it is time to go to bed you can utilise some of the nine ideas above in the title "Aim for a better quality of sleep".

2. **Know (and feel) your reason.** Think of something positive that you want to accomplish. Maybe you enjoy meditating but don't often have the time, so use that as a reason to get up and start your day!

3. **Think of it as a reward**. By rising early, you reward yourself. Remember that if you need a motivator you could also treat yourself with something nice if you manage to get out of bed on time.

4. **Plan to use the extra time.** Use the extra time you get in the morning to do something that helps you grow and progress. Maybe you crave the quiet time so that you can have the space and time to meditate? Perhaps there is a book you have wanted to read or an exercise class you have been wanting to attend?

5. **Don't eat before bedtime**. Eating may cause sleep disruptions of even nightmares. If you feel hungry before bed it's a better idea to have some herbal tea instead of a snack laden with carbohydrates.

6. **Decide to get up!** Be firm with your mind! Tell yourself the night before that you *are* getting up early. Put a reminder on your phone, on the fridge door, on your mirror, so that you are prompted.

7. **Set your alarm clock**. It is unlikely that you would wake up naturally at your goal time every morning, so set an alarm. Put it somewhere away from your bed so you have to get up to turn it off!

8. **Start slow**. Don't try suddenly getting up at 5am if you're used to getting up at 7:30. It is just too much of a change too soon. You are more likely to fail. You could try waking up 30 minutes earlier each day whilst your body gets used to the change. In a short time, you'll get there.

9. **Leave your bedroom.** Don't risk crawling right back to bed. Instead, head to the bathroom or the coffee machine so that you are awake enough to start the day.

In closing...

By now you can easily see that there are numerous benefits to getting up early and no negatives.

Why not try it for a week to test what sort of a difference it makes in your attitude, energy levels, and productivity?

Intuitively you know that you need quality sleep to function optimally. Think of times in your life when this knowledge has been borne out.

Can you improve your sleep quality and quantity to make a positive impact going forward?

CHAPTER 2
MEDITATION & RELAXATION

(and Work/Life Balance)

I have always had a 'fast' brain. It loves to do loops at various times, especially in stressful periods. It is annoying and frustrating when you can't calm your brain down. It is blissful when you can!

Instinctively I knew that one of the first things that I needed to do was give myself some peace and quiet in order to regain focus. I had heard that physical benefits will flow on from the mental benefits so it became a matter of finding out which type of meditation would work best for me.

These days there is a lot of talk about meditation and a number of famous celebrities are out there espousing the virtues of daily practice. There are a variety of different techniques - something for everyone – and highly worthwhile to explore. So, I investigated. I figured: if it is good enough for Hugh Jackman and Will Smith, it's good enough for me!

Do you know how many types of meditation there are?

One source told me that there are a staggering 23 main types!! That is mind-boggling in itself - and boggling is clearly *not* the object of meditation!

My advice: just start looking and you will find what you need. Remember the famous saying: ***"When the student is ready the teacher will appear!"***

Summary of the steps that I took around meditation and relaxation:

- **Pick a meditation technique and do it at least 3 times (or more) per week**
- **Listen to music**. There will be different music for different moods and states
- **Explore Hypnosis** – I have found this particularly beneficial as it assists you to get in touch with your inner self in order to create your future

- **Cut down on watching TV** … for so many reasons …!
- **Focus on Work/Life balance**: to achieve quality family time. Be present.

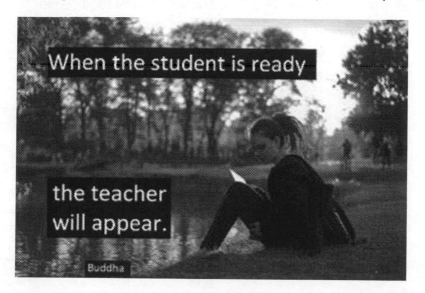

Meditate | Relax

Those who are experienced with meditation agree that a daily practice can have significant benefits for mental and physical health. However, they probably won't agree on which type is the most effective! There are myriad meditation techniques encompassing practices from different traditions, religions cultures and spiritual disciplines.

To simplify, the six basic types are:

Mindfulness meditation	Movement meditation
Mantra meditation	Visualisations
Guided meditation	Sound healing.

The table on the following page lists all the types under these basic headings. It is a breakdown of some of the more popular types of meditation.

Why so many kinds? That is simply because people are different and respond to things in their own unique way. There is no universally accepted "best" or "most effective" type. Rather, it comes down to our individual preference, so it is now time to get your exploration started and I hope that this helps you choose the one (or more) that works best for you.

It is a fascinating journey. Don't be in a hurry! You will find the one that works in your own time.

Types of Meditation	Examples
Concentration on a word, thought, sensation or image	Transcendental meditation Relaxation response Breath-focused meditation (Zen, Zazen) Mantra repetition Guided, Body Scan or progressive relaxation Sound healing Meditation on a prayer, mandala or other image.
Mindfulness	Mindfulness-based stress reduction Vipassana, Taoist,
Movement-based meditation	**Yoga** (particularly Kundalini, Kripalu, and Jivamukti), Tai Chi, Qi gong, Sufi dancing
Loving kindness/positive emotions meditation (such as compassion, forgiveness, gratitude).	Buddhist metta prayer or tonglen practices HeartMath training
Contemplative Prayer	Centring prayer, Waiting on the inner voice or inner light
* Some practices include more than one type of meditation, for example yoga may include meditation on the breath and a word or phrase or a sensation, and Taoist involves concentration, mindfulness, contemplation and visualisation.	

What do you get out of meditating?

Stress relief,
inner peace,
better sleep,
more confidence,
stronger sense of your spirituality,
better breathing technique,
greater ability to organise your thoughts,
more positive outlook on life (compassion, empathy, mindfulness),

a sense of calm,
relaxation,
self-awareness,
feeling centred,
tranquillity,
more connection,

All of these can assist weight management, detoxification, increased libido, relief of chronic pain, more strength, flexibility, and mobility.

Yoga Practice

Yoga is essentially a therapy and the techniques can be used to address physical injury, pain or mental and emotional stress and trauma. It can help you heal. Yoga has been around for thousands of years, and contrary to the Western way of thinking, traditionally, yoga has not been all about the pose. Yoga is about the breath, and simply mastering breathing can pay dividends when it comes to your health.

There are many types of yoga practice on offer. Listed below are the main ones that are most likely available to you at studios and clinics. It is a good idea to get a feel for all the different types of yoga before you attend a class. For instance, hatha yoga classes tend to be good for beginners because they are slower moving. Vinyasa, Ashtanga, and power yoga classes can be more challenging, depending on the level of instruction, although Vinyasa classes are frequently geared to beginners. Iyengar has a strong focus on proper alignment, and often uses props to help students perfect their form. Having said that, it doesn't matter too much where you start - just start and feel the benefits. Enjoy exploring the various types.

Ashtanga Yoga. Consists of six unvarying asana (pose) sequences that are to be practised in gradual progression. A great emphasis is placed on the connection between breath (pranayama), visual focus point (dristi), and the pose itself.

Vinyasa Flow. This mixes up asanas to create new and creative sequences. It is all about breath-movement connection — the poses flow from one to another in a fluid, almost dance-like manner on inhale or exhale. There might be music, props (such as blocks, straps, or pillows) and burning incense depending on a teacher's style – no two Vinyasa classes are the same.

An interesting and popular derivative on this is Jivamukti yoga. It is similar to vinyasa but is infused with Hindu spiritual teachings and chants that align to the philosophy. The emphasis is on connection to the Earth as a living being.

Iyengar Yoga. The aim to create balance in the body and mind and involves performing poses in a specific sequence in order to maximise their beneficial effects. A unique feature of Iyengar yoga is the use of props (such as blocks, pillows, chairs, straps, and bolsters) which provide support and help students balance, stretch, and attain perfect alignment in each pose. The poses can be standing, seated, or lying and may involve bends, twists, or inversions.

In addition to helping students gain flexibility, balance, and strength, Iyengar yoga may be useful in the management of certain health conditions like chronic lower back pain.

Bikram Yoga. A set sequence of 26 asanas (each done twice) performed in a hot and humid room. Extensive sweating allows tense muscles to soften so students can go deeper into each asana. It is also believed to promote detoxification and the flushing out of toxins.

Kundalini Yoga. Often referred to as "the Yoga of Awareness", this system combines asana, pranayama, meditation, and chanting designed to awaken the energy at the base of the spine and move it upward through the seven chakras to reach enlightenment. Kundalini sequences (kriyas) consist of asanas combined with a specific breathing technique designed to awaken a particular chakra. Each class will include a short opening chant, a warm-up sequence to improve spine flexibility, a kriya (asana sequence) and a closing meditation – it is a very powerful experience and can seem overwhelming or even emotional at first.

Yin Yoga. Based on the Taoist concept of yin and yang – yang representing athletic activities that generate heat in the body, while yin the softer, more restorative activities that heal the body. Yin yoga was designed to help go deeper than superficial muscular tissues and target the joints, ligaments, and bones through passive stretches and long posture holds.

Yin classes are slow in pace – the students go through asanas in meditative silence and stay in each posture between one and twenty minutes. The traditional Yin class has very little movement and consists of a sequence of 18 to 24 floor postures that are designed to strengthen the pelvic floor, release the hips and lower-back tension, and stimulate particular meridians (energy channels in the body).

Aerial/Swing Yoga. Also known as "anti-gravity yoga", this is a new style that started in New York as a fusion of traditional yoga asanas, Pilates, dance moves, calisthenics, and acrobatics elements practised using a hammock or swing that hangs from the ceiling.

DONNA PORTLAND

It is a fun and liberating experience – students float through poses that have been adopted for a hammock from the more traditional yoga styles, as well some new aerial-only asanas, such as the "Chandelier". Each class features inversions (which can be practised even by beginners with the swing support) that are great for decompressing the spine.

Hatha Yoga. Refers to the physical aspect of a yoga practice (asanas as opposed to meditation) that encompasses every yoga style out there – so both Bikram and Yin Yoga (as different as they may seem) can be grouped under the Hatha umbrella. Hatha is known as a slow and more gentle yoga with longer posture holds and no flow in between asanas. It builds a great foundation for more advanced and physically challenging styles, such as Ashtanga.

Tai Chi

Tai Chi is an art embracing the mind, body and spirit.

Originating in ancient China, tai chi is one of the most effective exercises for health of mind and body. Although an art with great depth of knowledge and skill, it can be easy to learn, and its health benefits will soon be evident.

The major styles and forms of tai chi are Chen, Yang, Wu, Wu (different words in Chinese) and Sun. Each style has its own features, but all styles share the same essential principles.

The essential principles include mind integrated with the body; control of movements and breathing; generating internal energy, mindfulness, song (loosening) and jing (serenity). The ultimate purpose of tai chi is to cultivate the qi or life energy within us to flow smoothly and powerfully throughout the body. Total harmony of the inner and outer self comes from the integration of mind and body, empowered through healthy qi through the practice of tai chi.

It is aesthetically pleasing, easy and enjoyable to practice. It can be a meditation and an integral exercise for all parts of the body and the mind. It brings tranquillity and helps you think more clearly. Tai chi can be many things for different people; regular practice will bring better health and wellness.

Numerous studies have shown tai chi improves muscular strength, flexibility, fitness, improve immunity, relieve pain, and improve quality of life. In a non-religious sense, it is a spiritual experience, satisfying beyond words, bringing those who practice into harmony with the world and nature.

To get the most benefits from tai chi you need to practice for at least fifteen minutes a day - every day! It is better to practice every day than to have longer tai chi workouts two or three times a week.

Explore Hypnosis

Hypnotherapists mostly use hypnosis to help people break bad habits like smoking and overeating, and also highly useful for anxiety and stress reduction, plus pain control. Perhaps the greatest value that hypnosis offers is that it can be used to assist healing in the body via by the activity of your unconscious mind which affects the conductivity of the neurotransmitters that surround all cells. You can learn self-hypnosis to transform and enhance yourself.

Hypnosis is a fascinating subject well worth exploring as it can offer many other important benefits; increased learning capability, unlocking your creativity, focusing your energy, and manifesting being of major value. The significance of this is that we can tap into our unconscious to understand ourselves, create our future and fulfil our dreams.

To clear up a common misconception hypnotherapy is *not* a form of entertainment for an audience! That is known as "stage hypnosis" and is often 'performed' by mentalists practicing their art form. The truth is that people will not cluck like chickens or remove their clothes on the stage by hypnotic suggestion unless they are the sort of person who might do those things anyway!

Hypnosis is a powerful transformational tool that you can utilise to effect positive change in your life! You, as the client, always have control of yourself.

Is hypnosis like meditation?

In general, the goal of meditation is to relax the body so that the mind can follow. Hypnosis often uses a similar approach to relaxation mainly via breathing, visualisations and 'deepeners' to achieve the trance state which is a very relaxing experience by itself. As such, meditations and hypnosis can be seen as quite similar as the body and the mind are deeply relaxed. Hypnosis takes this one step further. Via hypnosis you can communicate with your unconscious mind.

The secret of success is in creating rapport between the Conscious and Unconscious. Note that there is no distinction made between unconscious and subconscious. To hypnotherapists these are the same for all intents and purposes.

The father of hypnosis Milton Erickson said that hypnotherapy patients are people who have had too much (outside) programming - that they have lost touch with their inner selves. The

DONNA PORTLAND

idea being that people who are in rapport with their unconscious minds are also in control of their destiny. That's a big statement!

The secrets and benefits of hypnosis lie in the trance state which is a normal and natural state that you experience daily. It is not unusual or strange and it will feel vaguely familiar. Have you ever 'zoned out' and become aware that your mind went somewhere else for a while. It commonly happens when you drive, watch TV, ride an elevator, and listen to music. Without any intention on your part you go to your unconscious brain. It even happens in conversation. When people speak of hypnotic trance that are referring to a level of awareness that is different from your ordinary state of consciousness. It is a human condition involving reduced peripheral awareness, focused attention, and an enhanced capacity to respond to suggestion via communication with the unconscious mind.

The unconscious mind manages sensations and bodily functions and can communicate with every cell in the body. You do not consciously think about making your heartbeat or breathing or filtering your blood through your kidneys or how much glucose to convert to energy to get through your busy day. Your unconscious takes care of all this for you.

Please visit my website: www.DonnaPortland.com if you would like more information on Hypnotherapy. I studied to become a Hypnotherapist when I realised how powerful this modality can be, especially to get over your initial problems/blockages and gain some momentum toward fulfilling all areas of your life. For me, I was able to reduce stress, find clarity and maintain focus. I am now also pain-free*. (*Little caveat: Of course, one still needs to maintain regular exercise, good hydration, quality sleep and conscious diet to maintain a pain-free existence!)

Listen to Music (to relax or re-energise!)

I don't think that anyone needs much evidence to support the recommendation to listen to music! We have all felt how music can lift your soul or takes you back to a moment in time and evoke an emotion or two. You've been to parties or night clubs where the music is cranking, and the vibe is high-energy, and you are so energised by the music alone that you could stay up all night! At my gym I get particularly energised by the pump-up music they play. There is a funky techno mix of "I got the power" that keeps me striding, rowing, or cycling as the case may be. Clearly the fitness industry is well aware of the power of music when it comes to energising people!

Whenever I am in a down mood I switch on some upbeat music. My favourite is "Happy" by Pharrell Williams. It always livens me up and makes me feel good. It is part of the human condition that we all respond to the emotion of music and it has always been that way over the centuries – across all cultures.

The right music can make all the difference when you are trying to be productive.

Some days, you've just lost your mojo and it's hard to put some pep in your step and do your best. During these times music can be effective in keeping you alert and productive, but according to science, certain tracks might do a better job of revving you up any time you hit a slump.

Here is a brief explanation. Brain waves are electrical pulses that fire between masses of neurons, allowing those neurons to communicate with each other. Without wanting to get too bogged down into the science, it is the beta waves that scientists associate with everyday alertness, critical thinking, socialisation, learning and cognitive processing and gamma are the fastest during periods of extremely high functioning. [When you sleep you are using slow delta waves. Alpha and Theta waves are typically present when your brain is idling or in deep states of meditation.]

Research has found that rhythm serves as a type of carrier signal for information, where brain waves actually synchronise to the tempo of sounds around you, including music. Studies have found that the amplitude of beta waves went up as the music tempo got faster. Findings suggest that any music is stimulating and that listening to quicker tracks might be a legitimate way to coax your brain into a temporarily more active state.

You intuitively know what you respond to – so use it. Create a list of 'go to' songs that lift you up when you need it. Keep some, or all of these songs, in playlists on whatever device you prefer.

I'll confess that, due to my vintage, I am an 'eighty's tragic' so the theme music from Beverley Hill's Cop is one that gets me going. Whenever I need a pick-up I play it, or "Venus" (Bananarama) and various others. Don't judge: Just find the ones that work for you!

Find the music that will enhance your mood and state.

1. Music **increases happiness** - neurotransmitter (dopamine) release boosts your emotions.

2. Music **improves performance in running** – scientific tests confirm that music inspires, but you already know this intuitively!

3. Music **decreases stress** while increasing overall health – to counteract the effects of stress by decreasing the cortisol levels (the hormone related to stress) and some studies also showed a boost to the immune systems.

4. Music **improves sleep** – studies have shown that listening to classical or relaxing music within an hour of going to bed significantly improves sleep.

5. Music **reduces depression** by directly affecting our hormones – like a natural antidepressant! It can cause those neurotransmitters (serotonin and dopamine and norepinephrine) to release.

6. Music **helps you eat less.** Research reveals that the combination of soft lighting and music leads people to consume less food (and enjoy it more!). Excellent news!!

DONNA PORTLAND

7. Music **elevates your mood while driving.** Studies have found that listening to music positively influences your mood while driving, which obviously leads to safer behaviour and less road rage.

8. Music **strengthens learning and memory.** Research points to music helping you learn and recall information more efficiently, but it depends on the extent to which you like the music!

9. Music **increases verbal intelligence**. Studies showed that children between the ages of four and six had significantly increased verbal intelligence after only a month of taking music lessons, where they learned about rhythm, pitch, melody, and voice. The results suggest that the music training had a "transfer effect" that increased the children's ability to comprehend words, and even more, explain their meaning.

10. Music **raises IQ and academic performances.** Research suggests that taking music lessons predetermines high academic performance and IQ scores in young children.

Cut down on watching TV...

Has watching television become the default activity when you get home at the end of the day? Why not? it's easy. The problem here is that it is also passive, which means that you are not feeding your brain – you're just vegetating ...

I am not suggesting that there is nothing worth watching. There are indeed some programs that provide information and food for thought that have excellent value. However, there is also a lot of pulp that just fill hours. These are hours that you could have spent doing something positive, empowering, creative, healthy, and useful.

There is a place for chilling out in front of the television when you're tired and don't have much energy left to give, but generally it is wise to cut down on the amount of TV you watch as it will insidiously sap your time.

There are some stunning statistics revealed by polls on the amount of TV watching. According to data released by Nielsen in 2016, American adults watch an average of 5 hours and 4 minutes of television per day. That's *a lot* of wasted hours... I wonder if Australia is far behind?

The habit of watching television starts at a young age and unfortunately, in some families, the TV has become the unofficial nanny, keeping children glued to it while parents do things they need to do.

Another important point to make is that late at night the blue light that emanates from the screen will affect your ability to get off to sleep. There is also the hype and noise from some TV shows which can be disturbing, if not draining.

So, be selective as much of the content doesn't feed your brain and be discriminating about what you choose to watch. Does it really entertain? Does it really inform?

Many people think that the nightly News is depressing – I am one of them. I have received criticism about that opinion. It is not that I want to be ignorant about what is going on in the world. I do stay in touch but let's face it, The News that we are fed is usually a litany of *bad* news. I mostly choose to read online from a variety of sources to get a well-rounded perspective about topics of interest. I would also prefer to watch uplifting entertainment or do something active!

Here are a few ideas to ditch watching TV in favour of other activities:

Build a healthier self-esteem *(by removing the influence of constant marketing on TV: unrealistic expectations and comparisons!)*

Increase your productivity

> Focus on your social interactions
> instead of solitary activities

> > Sharpen your thinking processes

> > > Stop being sedentary: live healthier

> > Cancel your cable subscription
> > and save money

> Be a better role model for your
> children: do something productive
> or creative instead!

STOP WATCHING AS MUCH and find alternatives to the television!

> Wean yourself off.

> > Go cold turkey and just stop!

> > > Focus on healthier habits instead!

Focus on Work/Life balance:

Consider these statements:

What we think about is what we **FIND** time for.

What we care about is what we **MAKE** time for.

What we love we will **INVEST** time in.

We always find time, make time and invest time in *what matters to us.*

We **SAVE** time if we ditch what just **FILLS** time...*(like TV, for example)*

Where we SPEND our time will determine the quality of our lives.

We cannot expect to change that which we give **NO** time for.

So, what do *you* mostly think about? Care about? Love? and invest your time in? Take a careful look. Go to the extent of estimating the time you spend doing the various things you do and see where it is skewed. This reveals the truth about your work/life balance, your interests, and what matters to you most. It may even be confronting. It may not. It *will* be a useful exercise in any case. You will discover if you need to make changes to bring things back into balance.

Are you giving enough time to achieving quality family time? for relaxation and fun?

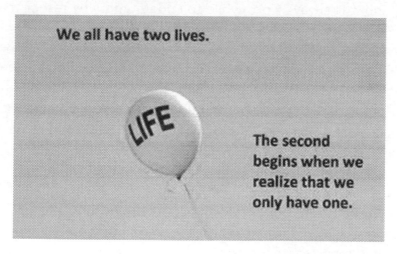

Attributed to Confucius

This is an amazing gift when you think about it......

CHAPTER 3
HYDRATION

Interesting fact: often we think we are hungry, but that feeling is actually brought on by being thirsty! You can imagine how this wrecks your efforts towards staying on a diet!

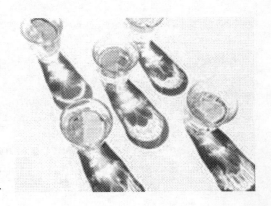

I discovered that this was my problem too. To my surprise I was told by various medical professionals that I was dehydrated. They said that if I wanted to improve my wellness I needed to drink more water every day.

So, my quest to enhance my health and vitality led me to explore the role that hydration plays. When you start to seek evidence for why you need to drink more water it is not difficult to find and it is always worthwhile to understand why rather than just accept the advice.

Why hydrate? The primary reason was that I wanted to feel better: to get rid of the lethargy, muscle weakness and headaches. I found that if I simply drank more water I could also improve the appearance of my eyes and skin (less wrinkling and dryness) and it also assisted in losing weight. I was sold. I decided to commit to drinking more water! It's free and it's easy!

Unfortunately, tea, coffee and alcohol do not count – they are diuretics (they cause your kidneys to excrete water from the body). Soft drinks are nutritionally useless: not only is the sugar content sky high but the ones with artificial sweeteners are just as problematic as the sugary ones! It is important to realise also that commercial juices are laden with sugar. This meant that I had quite a few changes to make! I needed to increase my water intake to around 2.5 litres or more of water per day. I needed to give my kidneys the water they require to effectively filter and detoxify my blood adequately.

The good news is that there are several water-based drinks that can help:

Warm water and Lemon Juice first thing in the morning. I read a lot about ways to feel better and improve my health. I knew that by boosting my physical health I would be boosting my mental health. One useful piece of advice I adopted comes from Ayurvedic traditions. This is to have a glass of warm water and the juice from half a lemon each morning upon waking.

Even though it is technically an acidic food lemon juice produces alkaline by-products once it has been metabolised and has an alkalinising effect on urine. Lemon juice is high in vitamin C a strong antioxidant and supports the immune system. Drinking vitamin C with meals may help increase absorption of some minerals. Antioxidants may also reduce the risk of heart disease, inflammation, and prevent the formation of some types of kidney stones. It is natural, inexpensive and it felt right to give it a try.

Herbs to promote mental clarity. By now you have come to understand that I chose to keep an open mind and try things that could work to contribute to a better quality of life. I also did not want to accept that memory loss, forgetfulness, 'senior moments' and possibly even Alzheimer's disease are part and parcel of aging. So, I looked into whether herbs could help stimulate the brain and enhance clarity. I researched until I found medicinal herbs that could lower stress and boost brain function. The blend that I use has gotu kola, bacopa, ginseng, lyons mane, ginger, lemon, cinnamon and gingko biloba. I drink my 'brain-mind-clarity tea' each morning after my initial lemon juice flush-out.

Since incorporating these two morning habits into my daily life I have definitely noticed the improvements to my general health. Headaches are rare. The lethargy has gone, and I feel more energetic. My eyes and skin are more vibrant. The excess weight that I carried slowly dropped off. Admittedly I have done other things (like improvements to my diet and exercise) to affect this, but I am positive that the increased water consumption has contributed in a big way.

If you are like me you may have to remind yourself all the time to drink water. I set alarms on my phone to remind me to drink – otherwise hours go by and I forget. I also have a water bottle in the car, on the desk, in the bathroom, bedside table, laundry, coffee table ... Works for me – and will for you too!

Here is a summary of the steps that I took around hydration.

It may be useful for you to add to your list of things to incorporate into your new set of daily habits.

- **Drink more water:** from 2½ - 3 litres of water per day - depending on your body size and the amount of activity you do. It may help to set reminders to drink water.

- **Drink lemon juice in hot water** each morning after waking to alkalinise the body and boost immunity.

- **Drink 'Mind-Brain herbal tea' each morning**: a blend of specific herbs known to enhance brain function. If you are time poor: Green Tea is an easy option.

More elaboration and information about dehydration if you're interested in the science.

Dehydration is a common problem contributing to a dis-eased state. Dehydration happens if we use and lose more water than the body takes in. It can lead to an imbalance in the body's electrolytes which help carry electrical signals between cells.

Remember that you lose water faster when the weather is really hot and you are sweating, when you are physically active, or if you have a fever. Vomiting and diarrhoea can also lead to rapid water loss. If you don't replace the water you lose, you can become dehydrated.

Recognising dehydration is important. Signs include:

- Little or no urine
- Urine that is darker than usual
- Dry mouth
- Sleepiness or fatigue
- Extreme thirst (note that, particularly in older adults, dehydration can occur without thirst!)
- Headache
- Confusion
- Dizziness or light-headedness
- No tears when crying
- Constipation
- Shrivelled and dry skin
- Lack of sweating (with severe dehydration)
- Low blood pressure

Actively prevent dehydration by drinking plenty of water. Do not wait until you notice symptoms of dehydration before you take action.

Water keeps you hydrated, and it's free!

Water is essential for the kidneys to function. Every day, the kidneys filter around 115-142 litres of fluid. Water helps dissolve minerals and nutrients, making them more accessible to the body. It also helps remove waste products. These two functions make water vital to the kidneys. Drinking plenty of water is a simple way to reduce the risk of damage to the kidneys and keep them functioning optimally.

Drinking water may also contribute to a healthy weight-loss plan. Some research suggests that drinking water can help you feel full. It worked that way for me.

Generally, you need 10-plus, (200ml/7oz.) glasses of water each day. It can be more for some people – depending on their body size and activity levels: from two to three litres per day

If you are concerned that you are not drinking enough water, check your urine. It should be colourless or light yellow, you are well hydrated. If your urine is a dark yellow or amber colour, you may be dehydrated.

Fruit and vegetable juices, milk, and herbal teas add to the amount of water you get each day. Watch out for drinks that contain caffeine or excess sugar: i.e. the so-called energy drinks.

If staying hydrated is challenging for you, here is a summary of tips that can help:

- Keep a bottle of water with you during the day. Reduce plastic waste and carry a reusable water bottle and fill it with filtered water (or from the tap if it is safe to do so in your particular area).

- If you have trouble remembering to drink water, drink on a schedule: drink lots of water when you wake up, and more between breakfast and lunch, and more between lunch and dinner, and in the evening before you go to bed. Alternately, drink a glass of water at the beginning of each hour. Set reminders to yourself if, like me, you forget!

- When you are feeling hungry, drink water. Thirst is often confused with hunger. You will soon find out because true hunger will not be satisfied by drinking water.

- Add a slice of lemon or lime to your water if you tire of the taste of plain water. Other additives could be orange, cucumber or mint.

- Make sure to drink water before, during, and after a workout.

- When you go to a restaurant or a bar, save yourself money (and a hangover) by having a drink of water between alcoholic drinks. Hangovers are caused by dehydration!

Lemon juice in hot water…alkalinises the body.

The Ayurvedic tradition of drinking a cup of warm water with lemon in the morning can radically alter your experience of the day. Try it for a month and do not be surprised if you begin to view mornings in a new light.

It helps to start the day on a hydrated note, which helps prevent dehydration and adrenal fatigue. When your body is dehydrated, or deeply dehydrated (adrenal fatigue) it cannot perform all of its proper functions, which leads to toxic build-up, stress, constipation, and so on.

Ayurvedic philosophies define perfect health as *"a balance between body, mind, spirit, and social wellbeing."* Ayurveda is all about getting a jump-start on the day by focusing on morning rituals that work to align the body with nature's rhythms, balance the energies (doshas) and foster self-esteem alongside self-discipline.

The benefits are:

- **A boost to your immune system**. Vitamin C is great for fighting off colds and the potassium stimulates brain and nerve function and helps control blood pressure.

- **Balancing pH.** Lemons are an incredibly alkaline food, believe it or not. Yes, they are acidic on their own, but inside our bodies they are alkaline (the citric acid does not create acidity in the body once metabolised). Wellness devotees will tell you that an alkaline body is really the key to good health.

- **Helps with weight loss.** Lemons are high in pectin fibre, which helps fight hunger cravings. It also has been shown that people who maintain a more alkaline diet lose weight faster.

- **Aids digestion.** The warm water serves to stimulate the gastrointestinal tract and peristalsis - the waves of muscle contractions within the intestinal walls that keep things moving. Lemons and limes are also high in minerals and vitamins and help remove toxins in the digestive tract.

- Acts as a **gentle, natural diuretic**. Lemon juice helps flush out unwanted materials because lemons increase the rate of urination in the body. Toxins are released at a faster rate which helps keep your urinary tract healthy.

- **Clears the skin**. The vitamin C helps decrease wrinkles and blemishes. Lemon water purges toxins from the blood which helps keep skin clear as well.

- Hydrates the lymph system.

Note that in Ayurveda, every individual is unique and there is no diet or lifestyle routine that works for everyone. This is why it's so important to truly search and try different things to find out what works best for you. Be in tune with your body and use your intuition.

Drink "brain-mind-clarity tea" each morning.

Many people believe that memory loss is an inevitable part of aging, but this is not necessarily true. Whether you are talking about occasional forgetfulness or a loss of short-term memory, it is important to understand that there are factors that can cause even younger people to experience episodes of memory loss. Some of the causes are due to drug or alcohol abuse, lack of sleep, stress, depression, overwork, prescription medications, stroke, nutritional deficiency, and head injuries.

Have you ever felt like your brain simply cannot meet your daily demands?

Do you sometimes feel that you forget things because your brain is basically overtaxed?

Do you think that your memory is weak?

Is concentration and focusing difficult for you?

If you have answered yes to any of these questions, then perhaps you could benefit from one or more of the herbs in the following list.[8] You may be able to protect your brain from excessive demands of the modern world and perhaps even protect it from brain related diseases, such as dementia or Alzheimer's disease, by trying some of the herbs that are known to improve the function of the brain. Medicinal herbs such as the ones in the list below have been known to help lower stress levels and enhance brain function.

Bacopa should be top on your list If you are looking for what is probably the most powerful memory improving herb known today! Numerous studies done on this herb show that bacopa has a powerful ability to improve both mental health and mental clarity. Bacopa has been used in Ayurvedic medicine since ancient times to improve concentration, learning abilities, and memory. One study conducted in Australia involved 46 subjects between the ages of 18 and 60. Divided into two groups, one group received a placebo; the other group was given 300mg of bacopa every day. After a period of 12 weeks, scientists discovered that the subjects who were given bacopa had vastly improved memory, speed of information processing, and verbal learning abilities.

Gingko Biloba. As you may know, gingko biloba supplements are one of the most popular herbal supplements these days. Gingko's ability to improve the memory is outstanding and scientific studies confirm that it can improve both memory and the thought process in those with dementia and/or Alzheimer's. It protects the nerve cells that have been damaged by these diseases, which improves learning, social behaviour, and reduces feelings of depression. Lab tests also show that gingko also improves blood circulation along the entire central nervous system, which promotes overall brain function.

---

[8] Please note that it is recommended you seek medical and/or naturopathic advice before taking any herbs or supplements.

Gotu Kola is amazing when it comes to improving brain function and memory. Used in both traditional Chinese and Ayurvedic medicine, this herb promotes the rejuvenation of the mind and body. It is considered by many to be an anti-aging herb. Studies show that gotu kola has certain compounds that increase the power of the brain and improve blood circulation to the brain itself, resulting in improved concentration and better memory.

Ginseng is another popular herb which lab studies have shown to be effective in helping with memory problems. Ginseng was shown to activate neurotransmitter activity that promotes memory improvement.

Rosemary is a herb with a woodsy pungent aroma, that is often used in cooking, and in traditional medicines that improve the memory. Rosemary has been shown in lab studies to have powerful antioxidant compounds that kill the free radicals that cause cell damage. In one study, using rosemary in aromatherapy was shown to reduce cortisol levels and anxiety. Combined with other essential oils, rosemary was shown to improve concentration and memory.

Green Tea has traditionally been used for hundreds of years and can be trusted to be both effective and safe. It has powerful antioxidant compounds, much like rosemary. Recent studies verify this benefit and extracts were shown to help protect the proteins and lipids from age related damage caused by oxidation. Studies suggest that green tea can protect the hippocampus of the brain from age-related decline. Even if memory problems can be linked to a specific cause, it is comforting to know that these issues can be reversed using some of nature's natural herbs that appear to be designed just for this purpose.

Ashwagandha. Although it is not well-known, this herb is really superior when it comes to brain function. It lowers the effects of stress and brain overload. Ashwagandha is the herb of choice to improve mental clarity and cognitive function and works wonders for nervous exhaustion and protecting the brain from cell deterioration.

Periwinkle is well-known for its antibacterial, antispasmodic, anti-cancer and sedative effects, but it is not as well-known for its ability to improve memory. The leaves and seeds of this plant contain a compound called vincamine, which is thought to be a precursor to vinpocetine, a blood thinner that improves the circulation of blood to the brain, which promotes better oxygen use. Vinpocetine is one of the most important ingredients found in most of the pharmaceutical drugs used for dementia and Alzheimer's disease. Vinpocetine is a powerful killer of free radicals, which prevents any damage to the blood vessels and prevents dementia. It also encourages the brain to absorb more nutrients, which will significantly improve the brain's function. Some researchers believe that periwinkle works in the same way that ginkgo biloba does to improve memory.

Peppermint is a common and popular herb stimulates the mind and has been shown in studies to improve learning abilities, creativity, and improve energy levels.

Blueberries are not herbs but are so powerful that they deserve a mention. Current scientific studies have found that blueberries contain powerful compounds that improve verbal comprehension, decision making, reasoning ability, cognitive function, and memory. Studies also show that consuming blueberries and their flavonoids regularly can help slow the decline of cognitive ability and offer protection from diseases such as Parkinson's and Alzheimer's.

Rhodiola Rosea. Although little-known this herb has a long history of use for various types of health problems and has been recognised by researchers and scientists as one of the best herbs for improving memory. This herb is sometimes called roseroot, golden root, or Aaron's rod and has traditionally been used to relieve depression and improve memory, as well as focus. It contains powerful adaptogenic compounds which stimulate the central nervous system, improving concentration abilities and concentration levels.

Sage is believed by scientists to contain compounds that boost chemicals in the brain that trigger faster transmission of messages in the brain. Research suggest that sage could offer benefits for those who are affected by Alzheimer's as it can boost the brain chemicals that drop off sharply with the onset of the disease.

Lion's mane mushrooms, also known as *hou tou gu* or *yamabushitake*, are large, white, shaggy mushrooms used in Asian countries like China, India, Japan and Korea, containing bioactive substances that have beneficial effects on the body, especially the brain, heart and gut. Studies have found that lion's mane mushrooms contain two special compounds that can stimulate the growth of brain cells and may help protect against Alzheimer's disease. Also that it has anti-inflammatory effects that can reduce symptoms of anxiety and depression.

Ginger may improve brain function and protect against Alzheimer's disease. Oxidative stress and chronic inflammation are believed to be among the key drivers of Alzheimer's disease and age-related cognitive decline. Some studies in animals suggest that the antioxidants and bioactive compounds in ginger can inhibit inflammatory responses that occur in the brain. Other studies show improved reaction time and working memory in humans and protect against age-related decline in brain function.

Cinnamon improves the body's ability to regulate blood sugar and this aromatic spice also boosts brain activity. Research shows that cinnamon to improve scores on tasks related to attention, memory and visual-motor speed. Also just smelling cinnamon enhances cognitive processing.

Studies on animals have found that cinnamon improved cognition and reduced oxidation in the brain and also that cinnamon protected dopamine production systems and improved motor function in Parkinson's disease.

CHAPTER 4

CONSCIOUS DIET

I knew that my diet was all sorts of wrong. It had to be, otherwise I would not have been so overweight and felt so lethargic! If my diet had been correct I would have been at my optimum weight and I would not have had so many headaches or cravings and I wouldn't have felt so exhausted so often. I needed to lose the 20-plus extra kilograms I was carrying. I wanted my skin to look radiant, my pain to go away and my energy to come back! So, I searched for the answers ...

Is this your story too?

What does your appearance (your body shape and your demeanour) reveal about your lifestyle and habits?

What story does it tell about you?

Diet: what a massive subject! There are so many differing points of view when it comes to choosing the right diet. The internet and bookshops are full of diet books. There are 'experts' galore, diets aplenty and weight loss companies in abundance, all with a different slant and all promoting their products ...

I wanted a healthy diet and did not want it to be complicated. Who has the time or interest to count calories or try to figure out complicated food combinations? I have tried that previously and found that it's just too hard – and therefore doomed to fail.

My goal was simple: I just wanted to look better and feel more energy and not have to lug around the equivalent of two enormous 10kg (22lb) dumbbells wherever I went!

I am living proof that these suggestions work to achieve your ideal weight. I followed my own advice. I am over 50 and I followed these steps. I am not perfect, but I stuck to the plan 80% of the time - and still do! That meant that I am able to have the occasional indulgence because, after all I *am* a "foodie" - I adore all foods. I have chosen to have some things in moderation - not give them up completely! Although I mainly eat a plant-based diet, I haven't claimed the label of 'vegetarian' and as don't believe in labels and also I didn't want to risk becoming socially isolated because of my dietary choices.

Photos taken two years apart.

WARNING: Achieving your goals – regardless of what they are – means that you need to make a commitment!

There's the rub...! Nothing happens unless you put in the work:
make a decision → define your goal
→ make a viable plan to reach your goal
→ TAKE ACTION every day and continue taking action every day!

The good news: pretty soon your new (healthier) habits are ingrained, and it feels like less effort to maintain them. Success breeds more success, not just on your initial goal but on other goals that you choose to focus on.

Conscious Diet: Simplicity is the Key.

I read widely, researched and did trials with my diet. In the end I came up with a simple regime that really works for me. It should work for you too. There is no rocket science here: it is simple to follow and not so prescriptive that you end up failing.

These are the seven main principles of a conscious diet:

1. **Eat organic** - to the largest extent possible. There are more useful nutrients in organic produce (and meat).

2. **Keep it fresh and unprocessed**: aim for around 70% of UNPROCESSED vegetables and fruit on your plate. That means as much raw as you can manage. (Tinned foods are next to useless.) **This is the basis of your nutrition and will have the greatest effect on reaching your optimal body weight.**

3. **Eat less volume of food.** It is obvious why! If you wean yourself off the quantity of food that you currently eat, you will soon get used to eating less.

4. **Cut out sugar** to the extent you can as it seems to have found its way into almost everything you can buy! The obvious things to cut out are confectionary, ice-cream, cake, and cookies. Wean yourself completely off *adding* sugar to your tea and coffee. The main reason for this is that sugar weakens your immune system, quite apart from being empty calories that cause energy highs and lows and keep the weight on.

   You won't miss the sugar if you chew your food well. You will feel more satisfied and will be able to taste more sweetness in your food when you chew for longer. So, do not rush through a meal - take the time to enjoy your food and this will also aid in your digestion.

5. **Cut down on meat.** We all eat far too much meat! It is not necessary. Our adult bodies simply do not need so much protein. *Protein can be gotten from plant-based foods in any case.*

   I will occasionally eat red meat, but probably only if served at a dinner party or in a lovely restaurant where it has been cooked to perfection by a talented chef! I have cut out chicken though, unless it's organic and free range. I just don't trust that it's not pumped full of hormones! I stick to steamed or baked fish and avoid tuna and swordfish as those fish have been known to contain mercury from the ocean. The safest fish, in terms of not having heavy metal content, are: Salmon, Mackerel, Anchovies, Sardines and Herring. The easiest was to remember that set of fish is to use the acronym SMASH.

6. **Avoid dairy food.** Dairy is not necessary - unless it is for a calf! Human adults do not need milk. It has taken me a long time to change my habits around dairy as I was brought up on it! There are a wide variety of dairy substitutes if you are used to adding milk to beverages. I steer clear of dairy because it causes congestion. Be aware that some soy milk[9] manufacturers use genetically modified soybeans, so be careful to choose the safe brands of soy milk or stick to almond, coconut, oat, rice, or macadamia milk.

   Probably the hardest thing for me about avoiding dairy is that I love cheese! Remember that adhering to a conscious diet does not mean that you cannot ever have cheese, but best to save that indulgence for special occasions!

7. **Avoid fried foods** as the application of heat to oil completely changes its properties and it is simply not good for the body. The best source of oil is cold-pressed: olive, macadamia, Udo's oil (omega 3, 6,9) and you can even use this for salad dressing.

   If you are interested to learn more about oil, explore the work of Dr Udo Erasmus, who is an expert on the subject. It's fascinating!

Other things that impact whether you lose weight or keep stacking it on:

1. **Don't snack.** Most of the foods that you choose to snack on are just adding to your calorie count and/or sugar levels. You do not *need* more food than your basic meals, so when you feel peckish, drink a large glass of water instead - or herbal tea.

   Wheatgrass shots are great, in terms of nutrition, but you will need a source of fresh wheat grass and a good quality cold press juicer. It should be pressed and consumed on the same day - preferably straight after pressing. Wheatgrass is also much sweeter tasting that way. It goes a little bitter if you leave it a day. If you find the taste too strong you can add some pear or apple.

   Shots of "Udo's oil" (omega 3,6,9) are also powerful as a health booster.

   Don't overdo nuts or dried fruit. If you need to chew something that is not going to add to your calorie count try celery – but don't add a whole tub of hummus or some other kind of dip!

2. **Remove or reduce Toxicity from your life.** Think about what poisons you may be affected by, i.e. *excess* caffeine, nicotine, other drugs, aluminium (in your deodorant and/or from your Amalgum fillings), the chemicals in artificial sweeteners, artificial colourings, saturated oils, trans fats, heavy metals (i.e. mercury - from some ocean fish, sugar, preservative chemicals ...), parabens, air quality ...

---

[9]   *Intensive farming has used GM on soy and corn.*

3. **Plan your meals. Keep it simple.** In the beginning when I made some big changes I did not want to be always thinking about food: shopping, preparing, and cooking, so I tried a few home delivery meal services. It is important to try some out to see which you like and that suit you best. There are some excellent vegetarian ones offering tasty meals. I figure that if I am being conscious at least 80% of the time I am so far ahead of how I used to eat, and the results are obvious to me in how I look and the way I feel.

4. For breakfast I have a freshly squeezed fruit and vegetable juice or a "Brain Power Smoothie". I use almond/coconut milk as a base. There are lots of variations and you can use any combination of fruits: blueberries, raspberries, strawberries, pineapple, avocado, mixed berries, banana, grapes, pear, mango, protein powder (pea based) if you want to add it, chia seeds (makes it bulky and filling and breakfast will last you until lunchtime!) You can even throw in baby spinach and not notice the taste of the raw leaves amongst the other goodies.

5. **Distract yourself.** If you are obsessing about food ... and this always tends to happen when you start any new dietary regime, you will need to distract yourself. Keeping busy was important to me, so that 'bored eating' behaviour would not kick in! After a while you get used to the changes which have become your new habits!

6. **Consider Hypnosis:** If weight loss is a big issue for you, and you struggle with intrinsic motivation and will-power then consider getting help from a Hypnotherapist to kickstart you along the path. Note: There is more about Hypnosis in Chapter 2.

   Do not fall for the misinformation or hype about hypnosis that seems to be a common misconception. It is a powerful transformational tool that you can utilise to effect positive change in your life! Your problems won't magically evaporate away, but hypnosis will help you to deal with things more effectively and allow you to get some wins that you can feel good about and build momentum towards your end goal. By using the power of your unconscious mind, you will be able to:

   - Control your urges
   - Change your habits around food
   - Achieve your weight loss goals
   - Gain back your energy!

I studied and became a Hypnotherapist when I realised the power of this modality. If you would like more information on Hypnotherapy please visit my website: www.DonnaPortland.com

CHAPTER 5
EXERCISE

Life can be very limiting when you are overweight. There are things you cannot do – or just can't be bothered to even attempt doing! As I had gotten heavier and more lethargic, I was less and less inclined to move my body. I hated that way my body looked so I hid it. I bought "fat clothes": flowing, loose, nothing that tucked in... you get the idea. I went into denial. I did my hair, nails, make-up so on, but the most obvious thing that would have made the most impact on how I looked - my body - was denied. When I look around I realise how many people are exactly like this.

How do you fix it? The prescription is to make a new positive habit that will benefit your body and your mind. **Just start.** Make a commitment to yourself, make changes and keep on going!

I reached the point where I could not deny it any longer.

My habits around exercise needed to change. I had started doing the right thing with my diet, so I committed to doing the right thing with exercise. I knew that the results I wanted would follow if I just got started and stuck to it – kept putting one foot in front of the other. I admit – it is hard to start, but it does get easier as you go, and keep going.

I used to wake up late because I had stayed up late the night before watching TV, drinking wine, eating paté and crackers, ice-cream and chocolate ... These are clearly some seriously bad habits if you want to have a svelte body! I occasionally moved my body but nothing that could be described as regular exercise. I felt groggy when I woke up. My joints were felt stiff and creaky and I did not feel rested or energised when I woke. I could barely utter a "good morning" ...

Reiterating a crucial truth that was put forward in the last chapter regarding goals:

> # Achieving your goals and dreams means making a commitment!
>
> Nothing will happen unless you step up and put in the work:
>
> → make a **decision**
>
> → define your **goal**
>
> → make **viable plans and strategies** to reach your goal
>
> → **TAKE ACTION** every day and **continue taking action** every day!

It all changed when I decided to raise my standards: to get up early every day to walk and breathe some fresh air. That is how I started. I had been having trouble sleeping and found myself waking very early and being unable to go back to sleep. So, I thought 'why not go for a walk'? It is relatively easy and would help me to clear my head and was something positive I could do for myself. It was summer so it wasn't so difficult to do. I then made it a 'must do' every day. I walked for a good hour and worked up a sweat and a bit of puff. It helps to have good comfortable supportive shoes for the purpose.

It helps to have a walking buddy, or a dog. I took my dog with me, and he enjoyed our morning walks very much.

The wonderful thing about incorporating exercise into your life is that it really doesn't matter what you do as long as you do something! Of course, you get told all sorts of things from 'experts' about how a particular exercise regime will achieve this and other exercise regimes will achieve something else ... However, the fact is that it really comes down to just two simple things:

(a) **Move the body** to get your heart rate up, get the blood circulating and the joints lubricated.

(b) Get some momentum going, so that it becomes **a daily habit** to expend energy.

It's not a big deal what you start with – or what you do next. Just do something that achieves (a) and (b) above!

In the beginning I had fitness tracker which counted my steps and the goal was to reach a minimum of 10,000 steps in a day. I discovered that my normal day of just working at the desk in the office and coming home would be around 4,000 steps. So, when you add purposeful steps to your day it is fun to try to beat your record or at least maintain the required level. Sometimes, it would get to 11:30pm at night and I would realise that I still needed to clock up another 1000 steps, so the dog was a big winner as he would get a sneaky late-night walk. Not surprising that after while I noticed that the dog had lost weight too!

I found it quite motivating to feed my fitness tracker. I remember the day that I cleaned out the garage and did over 27,000 steps! It's quite motivating. After a while you won't need the tracker, as I discovered when I lost mine. By then I already knew what it took to do 10,000 steps a day!

When the weather started to get cooler and the days shorter I decided that it would be easier for me to maintain my exercise if I were to move it indoors to a gym for a while. So, I tried a weights regime next. My gym instructors were wonderful in coaching me with the correct body alignment and technique to get the most from the exercise without damaging myself. This is very important because many a gym goer gives up after they injure themselves.

Over the three-month winter period in the gym I got really strong and I also enjoyed the change of scene. I was able to get my BMI to the correct level – for the first time in my life since adolescence!

When I moved house I discovered cycling. The new area was a lot flatter and since I was given an old bicycle I thought I would give it a try and found that I really enjoyed the change. I was also living near a beautiful and enormous park which was safe for riding and I still do this. I barely needed to drive which was a positive change on many levels.

In the new suburb I found a different gym with a cardio emphasis, so changed things up again: this time it was more about workouts on the treadmill and the rowing machines. Since I enjoy variety and like to keep things interesting, I do a mixture of these depending on the season: walking, Pilates, yoga, stand-up paddle boarding, hiking, cycling, weights/gym, skiing, swimming...

If you cannot manage an hour a day, even 20 minutes will make a big impact on your health and well-being. So, do what you can to keep it interesting and varied, but **make it a daily habit.**

Try some High Intensity Interval Training (HIIT) workouts. These are short duration exercises aim to get heartbeat up. It can be as short as five minutes but better if you can go for twenty mins or longer. This could even be a vigorous dance to your favourite music to energise yourself! In fact, there are some great dance based HIIT workouts available if that appeals.

Try ditching the car, bus or train and walk to work or part of the way. This will increase your daily steps.

Walk and talk: Instead of meeting a friend for a coffee and sitting down in the café or meeting them in a bar and drinking glasses of wine, suggest that you meet up to go for a walk instead. You could even bring your coffees with you! I enjoy meeting a range of different friends for either a brisk walk, or a cycle. You can still chat, but you are using your time efficiently *and* it's fun!

These days I wake up feeling energised. I can't wait to get going. It is hard work at the gym, and I admit that I do have to make myself go, but I feel great afterwards and it sets me up for a good day. It has become a positive addiction. When I go to bed at night I am physically tired, and I sleep well. Interestingly also, I do not feel stiff and creaky anymore.

> Be aware that when it comes to weight loss it is more about **INPUT than OUTPUT.**
>
> **What you eat**
> (in terms of type, quantity and quality)
> has more effect than the energy
> you expend exercising so
> **diet needs to be your <u>primary</u> focus
> if you want to lose weight.**

CHAPTER 6

OTHER USEFUL DAILY HABITS

I have put into play a few other highly useful ideas that I have discovered relating to the physical body and its environment.

De-clutter your home.

Right off the bat I decided to de-clutter my living space. My grandmother used to say that there were enormous benefits to be gained from organising one's living space to be clean and orderly. The reasoning was that you would feel less stress in your mind if your physical space were organised. It was worth a try, so I started with my wardrobe and tossed everything I hadn't worn in years. I wound up donating loads of things to charity: clothes, shoes, bags, costume jewellery, books, etc. It felt wonderful - cathartic even.

It felt so good that I continued doing this throughout the house! I downsized the number of things I had stored. Grandma was 100% right: I really did not need all that 'stuff'. I make it a habit now to give away things that I don't need or don't use. Every couple of months I decide what needs to go. I have realised that someone else may really benefit from things that I no longer need. There are several platforms where you can give things away, swap or sell. I have discovered various Facebook groups in my city. I am sure that similar groups exist everywhere.

Use less power.

There are loads of ways you can reduce your electricity bill and be kind to the environment.

- Wear more layers in winter, plus socks and slippers, instead of sitting around in a T-shirt and bare feet with the heating cranked up.
- Fans in summer use less power than air-conditioners. Allow the breeze to come through the open window.
- Cooling down at the beach is free!
- Cycle or walk instead of drive.
- Switch off lights, appliances, and fans around the house when you're not there.

- Buy more energy efficient appliances when its time to replace old ones.
- Consider replacing your old petrol or diesel car with a hybrid or an electric car. (I am happy to say that I've recently done this, and it feels satisfying!)
- Use energy efficient light bulbs.
- Use the cold cycle on your washing machine and detergent designed for cold water.
- Turn down thermostats on water heaters.

Decide to enjoy what you already have.

I get such a great feeling from this and spend a lot less! By regularly cleaning out the cupboards I find things I thought I'd lost, and I discover things I'd forgotten about and find more opportunities to give things away to people who might want or need them.

Make your bed daily.

This was grandma's other big piece of advice, the idea being that it sets you up for the day and gives you a kind of 'organisational momentum'. I gave it a try and it works for me. I love coming home to a neat bedroom.

Use your non-dominant hand more!

Try brushing your teeth - morning and night – using your other hand, as this creates new neural pathways. It's good to encourage more ambidexterity! Your brain is just like a muscle and will improve through stimulation. If you don't use it, you lose it. So, do whatever you can to stimulate your brain and operate outside your comfort zone.

Consume less, Recycle and Repair.

When appropriate, instead of throwing things away and buying new, it makes sense to repair or recycle. It is also worth asking yourself "do I really need this?" and decide to consume less. You will also save a lot of money that way! Buy less and spend less.

......

CHAPTER 7
ENERGISE YOURSELF

You often hear people lament: *"Where did all my energy go ...?"*

When I was young I had boundless energy. I was always charging forward. My brother nicknamed me 'Road Runner'! But as I got older I noticed that I only seemed to wind down in the energy stakes.

Of course, our state of mind greatly affects how we feel. Many of us pay lip service to wanting to live our lives at 100% - at full capacity! But do we? **Two of the biggest complaints these days seem to be about not having enough time and not having enough energy.** I am sure that you can relate. At the end of the day you usually don't have much left to give.

Why is having energy so important?

Energy and vitality make us feel good and fuels our

Motivation to **Focus**, to

Achieve and **Accomplish**,

Take Action, **Reach** our **Goals**, and maintains our

Resolve and **Strive** forward.

This feeds into

Performance,

Productivity,

Passion,

Pursuing purpose,

Personal power.

Lack of energy (lethargy) on the other hand, stymies our resolve and the likelihood that we'll take any action or follow through. When your energy levels are down you just can't be bothered ... We all know how debilitating that can be, and the result is that nothing much ever gets done.

Scottish businessman, Andrew Carnegie has been quoted as saying:

> "The average person puts only about 25% of his energy and ability into his work. The world takes off its hat to those who put more than 50% of their capacity and stands on its head for the few and far between souls who devote 100%."

So, don't feel too bad if you're not putting in between 50 – 100% to your work. You have plenty of company!

Of course, the feeling of being energetic is both physical *and* mental. In the latter half of this book we will look at the mental aspects, but for now the focus is on the physical aspects.

It makes perfect sense to say that one's diet contributes the most to their physical resources and clearly our energy levels are affected by what we eat. You know this intuitively, and since this is such a huge physical contributor to our energy levels, diet has been covered in a previous chapter. For now, we will concentrate on the physical and practical habits that will contribute to, or reduce, your energy and how you can make some positive changes to get back on track towards living a vital and energetic life!

How *do* you get back your energy and vitality?

Here are some ideas:

1. Breathe Deeper

This point is first for a very good reason. The simple action of getting extra oxygen to your brain reenergises you quickly when you need it. Far better to do some simple breathing techniques than drink another coffee or go for another sugar hit. These may seem like they work to boost you up, but it is short lived and the longer term 'side effects' of those substances are harmful.

One of the best ways to lower stress in the body is to breathe deeply. When you breathe deeply, the message to your brain is "calm down and relax" and this affects your whole body.

Breathing exercises are a good way to relax, reduce tension, and relieve stress because they make your body feel like it does when you are already relaxed: decrease your heart rate, and your respiration rate as well as your blood pressure.

The good news is that breathing exercises are easy to learn and can be done whenever and wherever you are. Best of all you don't need any special equipment to do them!

There are a few ways you can breathe to relax and reenergise.

Relax: Belly Breathing

Do this easy exercise whenever you need to relax or relieve stress.

1. Sit down in a comfortable position or lie down flat.
2. Put one hand on your belly just below your ribs and the other hand on your chest.
3. Through your nose take a deep breath in and let your belly push out your hand. Your chest stays still and doesn't move.
4. Breathe out through your mouth - almost like you are whistling. The hand on your belly will go in and push all the air out.
5. Belly breathe from five to ten times and take your time with each breath.
6. Notice how you feel at the end of the exercise.

Relax: Roll breathing

This helps you to focus on the rhythm of your breathing and develop full use of your lungs. It can be done in any position, but perhaps it is best while you are learning to lie on your back with your knees bent.

1. With your left hand on your belly and your right hand on your chest breathe in and out and notice how your hands move.
2. Fill your lower lungs by breathing so that your belly (left) hand goes up when you inhale, and your chest (right) hand remains still. Do these ten times: breathing in through your nose and out through your mouth.
3. Then add the second step: Breathe slowly and regularly, inhaling first into your lower lungs as before, and then continue inhaling into your upper chest. As you do so, your right hand will rise, and your left hand will fall a little as your belly falls.
4. Make a quiet, 'breathing sound' as you exhale slowly through your mouth, as your left hand and then your right-hand fall. Feel the tension leaving your body as you exhale and become more and more relaxed.
5. Practice this way for up to five minutes and notice that the movement of your belly and chest rises and falls like the rolling motion of a wave.

   Notice how you feel.

Practice roll breathing daily until you can do it almost anywhere. It can be used as an instant relaxation tool whenever needed.

Take Care: You may feel dizzy the first few times they try roll breathing. If you begin to feel lightheaded or find that you breathe too fast, just slow your breathing. Remember to give yourself time and get up slowly.

Re-Energise: Morning breathing: "roll ups"

When you first rise in the morning try this exercise to relieve muscle stiffness and clear clogged breathing passages. Also use it to relieve back tension throughout the day.

1. Stand with feet hip-distance apart and bend forward from the waist with knees slightly bent. Let your arms dangle to the floor.
2. Whilst inhaling slowly and deeply, roll up slowing to return to a standing position, lifting your head last.
3. Hold your breath for just a few seconds when you reach the standing position.
4. Return to the original position exhaling slowly as you bend forward from the waist.
5. Try this at least three times.

   Notice how you feel.

Re-Energise: "Tactical Breathing" in "1-2-4" ratio

You can try "2-4-8" breathing or "4-8-16" breathing!

Do this exercise standing, sitting, or lying down. Use belly breathing technique as above.

1. Put one hand on your belly and the other on your chest as in the belly breathing exercise.
2. Take a deep, slow breath from your belly, and count to 2 (or 4) as you breathe in.
3. Hold your breath, and count from to 4 (or 8)
4. Completely empty your lungs as you breathe slowing whilst counting to 8 (or 16).
5. Repeat 5 to 10 times or as long as it takes until you feel calmer.

   Notice how you feel at the end of the exercise.

Take Care: If you feel dizzy the first few times you try this then stop, sit down and wait for the dizziness to pass. You will become used to this new way of breathing when you continue to do it.

Re-Energise: "Arm Pump"

This is a quick 30 second to one-minute exercise that is highly effective in getting your blood pumping and your breathing faster! Make some room and do this exercise standing but leaning forward with one of your feet at least a 30cm (12 inches) in front of the other so that you have a solid base. Put your arms in 'running' mode (elbows bent).

1. Pump one hand forward – fist towards your chin, whilst the other goes back – elbow first. Then bring the back fist forward and the other elbow back – like you're running.
2. Do this in rapid succession for 30 seconds whilst you puff in and out on each hand pump.
3. Keep it going as fast as you can and try for the full minute if you can manage the 30 seconds!

Take Care: If you feel dizzy the first few times you try this then stop, sit down, and wait for the dizziness to pass. You will become used to this exercise when you continue to do it and you will find that it really helps to 'rev you up'.

Re-Energise: Fast Breathing

For a much greater energy increase that also gets rid of mucous you can try this technique – also known as "bellow breathing". Please note that if you have any health condition that may be affected by this, i.e. high blood pressure, heart problems, ulcers, hernia, pregnancy, or recent surgery, please consult your doctor as it would be wise to be cautious.

This is breathing with forceful inhalation and exhalation so that breathing is not shallow. The diaphragm moves very quickly. Your respiration rate increases from the usual 15 – 18 breaths per minute to 30 to 100 breaths per minute. You can start low and gradually, over about 25 – 30 days, in order to increase to 100. We normally breathe in and out using 600 c.c. of lung capacity but our lung capacity is 6000, and we want to get closer to that using this type of breathing.

How to:

With your spine erect, with sit or stand. Personally, I find it easier to stand.

Shoulders are relaxed (not raised) during the sequence.

Your tongue is on the roof your mouth, right behind teeth. Keep it there the whole time.

Place hands on your lower abdomen to assure that it is moving, and not the chest.

- Of all the methods of increasing energy when tired, I find this one the most effective.

Take Care: If you feel dizzy the first few times you try this then stop, sit down, and wait for the dizziness to pass. You will become used to this exercise when you continue to do it and you will find that it really helps to 'rev you up'.

Variation 2: A variation of this has been popularised by Anthony Robbins and he calls it 'priming'. You could say that it is his personal version of an ancient yoga technique called Kapalabhati Pranayama breathing.

Robbins maintains that since 70% of the toxins inside of your body are removed through the lungs and since these days we're using less and less of our lung capacity, it necessary to maintain your body's optimal health, and oxygenate your cells through proper breathing.

To quote Robbins: *"Breath is the key to physical and mental well-being, and if done properly, it can boost energy, relieve pain, and transform our lives."*

This makes perfect sense and works for me. In Robbins' version, he does three sets of 30 with brief breaks in between. This can further be broken down into three sets of ten repeated three times. When you start to learn the exercise, you can begin with three sets of ten and work your way up. The exercise should leave you feeling energised.

You only need to visit YouTube to find a version of Robbins' Daily Priming exercise. I highly recommend trying it because he takes you through not only the breathing, but also gratitude, connection, and visualisation, so it is a powerful and highly useful tool.

Variation 3: If you prefer a less vigorous, but still effective technique, that operates along similar lines, you could try this version entitled "The 30 Second Breathing Exercise" created by Lifehacker Australia. Try it in the morning, or even in the mid-afternoon if you are starting to wilt. This quick breathing exercise boosts your energy and helps your brain wake up.

Method: Find a quiet spot like an unused room or corner if you are in the office. Rest your arms gently at your sides, stand up straight and close your eyes. Inhale deeply through your nose and raise your arms above your head. Take a deep breath and feel your rib cage expanding. Exhale fully and lower your arms. Repeat this for 30 seconds. It doesn't need to be as fast as Robbins' method. You can do this exercise for longer of course, but 30 seconds will give you the right effect if you don't have much time or privacy. Here is the link: https://www.lifehacker.com.au/2016/11/energise-yourself-with-this-30-second-breathing-exercise/

2. Music – to re-energise (or relax)

Music is relevant to list here, but since it was covered in Chapter 2, you can refer back to re-read if you would like to refresh.

3. Indulge in creative pursuits to re-energise

The dictionary defines creativity as 'The use of imagination or original ideas to create something; inventive.' It can be channelled in many different ways, not just through arts and crafts, on a sketchpad or a canvas. I find creativity in arranging flowers, styling my home, planning an event, gardening, designing an outfit, planning a holiday, arranging music, renovating, choosing and wrapping gifts, and even finding an elegant solution to a problem! By using a variety of medium and colour you can turn your imagination into a tangible thing.

You can also enjoy 'down time' when you can rejuvenate your body and mind. You can explore those parts of yourself you may never have met: the part that can draw or paint, sculpt or photograph. I find joy picking up the pencils, the paintbrush, or the camera. Art was one of my favourite subjects at school and it was great to experience a learning process that used a side of your brain that rarely gets to run free. Sadly, these days it seems that the education system is more focussed on scores and grades which, in my opinion, is skewed and does not give a well-rounded education to students.

Everyone has a creative side. Here is why you *should* explore your creative side.

There is a lot of useful information and research out there on the benefits of expressing and exploring your creative side and not only that, appreciating it so those benefits may be felt. The study 'Everyday Creative Activity as a Path to Flourishing' (Conner 2018), concluded that engaging in a creative activity just once a day led to a more positive state of mind which could have positive outcomes on other aspects of your life. Conner even expressed surprise: *"Research often yields complex, murky, or weak findings. But these patterns were strong and straightforward: Doing creative things today predicts improvements in well-being tomorrow. Full stop."* [10]

Studies do have limitations and in this case there was a reliance on participants' own reports of their experiences. It is not strictly possible to measure how creative people actually were, but nevertheless, it is quite clear that even if you think you've been creative, you can experience positive emotion. So, now embrace whatever ways you are creative in your job or leisure time!

"Every artist was first an amateur"

- Ralph Waldo Emerson

---

[10] Ref: 'Everyday Creative Activity as a Path to Flourishing' - Conner (Nov. 2016)

Sadly, many people think that being creative involves painting a masterpiece, like Rembrandt, so they don't try because they feel like they will fail. The truth is that even the greatest artists had their learning curve before the created their most inspiring work!

When I told friends that I go to art classes or drawing nights I heard so many reactions along the lines of "*I can't draw*" or "*I can't paint*", and "*I'm not artistic*", etc. etc. Of course you can't - if that is what you're always telling yourself!

Why not have a go? Leave your judgements at the door and do it anyway regardless of whether you are talented or average! Just do it because it feels good to explore and unlock that side of yourself. I admit that it is hard to let go of judgements when you examine your work, but this is what you *must* do to the extent possible. It is not about being perfect or an accomplished artist. It is about making a start on a wonderful path, giving it a try, and feeling how it expands you.

I can honestly say that brush in hand, hours fly, and you completely lose yourself in front of the canvas.

Take advice from the masters and give yourself permission:

"Creativity takes courage"

- Henri Matisse

Everyone has elements of creativity in them, but many do not give themselves permission to explore this side of themselves. Creativity just needs a little courage and an outlet – something that you enjoy doing that feels like fun.

To be creative,
firstly you need an idea
and then you need to act on it!

It's the same for anything
that you want to achieve
in life:
decide on what you want, make a plan
and then do it.

"Art enables us to find ourselves and
lose ourselves at the same time."
Thomas Merton

"Art washes away from the soul
the dust of everyday life."
Picasso

"A picture is a poem without words."
Horace

"You don't take a photograph, you make it."
Ansel Adams

"To use our creativity and imagination,
even in simple ways, is an affirmation of life."
Sam Lehane

"The only unique contribution that we will ever make
in this world will be born of our creativity."
Brené Brown

"I am enough of the artist to draw freely
upon my imagination.
Imagination is more important than knowledge.
Knowledge is limited.
Imagination encircles the world." [11]
Albert Einstein

---

[11] Quoted from an interview with George Sylvester Viereck and Albert Einstein in The Saturday Evening
Post, October 26, 1929.

DONNA PORTLAND

Some of the benefits include:

Feeling pride in your achievements and having something tangible to show for the time and effort.

Being able to make something unique for special people in your life - something that shows that you focussed on them and spent time lovingly creating your gift.

Reducing your stress or anxiety and lifting your mood.

The downside: of NOT being creative

We all experience how 'life gets in the way' of doing so many things ... Expressing your creativity is only one of those. Life becomes all about your responsibilities and important aspects of your self-expression and life-learning are often lost amid the scramble to earn money, parent, climb the career ladder, family responsibilities and so on.

There is a downside to this. Research Professor Brené Brown[12] has been quoted as saying that **'Unused creativity is not benign. It metastasizes. It turns into grief, rage, judgment, sorrow, shame. We are creative beings. We are by nature creative.'**

I highly recommend reading more of Brené Brown's work. Her research conclusions are particularly insightful, and she is an engaging speaker as well.

Studies have revealed that people are generally dissatisfied that they are not living up to their creative potential and wish they could be creative more often.

How you CAN be more creative

- Consult your calendar and pick a time soon to spend 15 minutes (maybe more) doing something creative that interests you.

- Schedule more time next time!

- Join a class - make it fun - bring a friend. I have heard of painting classes involving wine and cheese! I go to life-drawing classes with live models.

- Look for opportunities: style a room, plant a rockery, arrange flowers, dress the dinner plate like you're a chef in a restaurant, set the table using a centrepiece or theme, decorate a cake, compile a photo keepsake book (they make awesome gifts), keep looking for more possibilities!

---

[12] https://brenebrown.com

One of my greatest wishes is to one day create a studio/ sanctuary where busy people could come and take off their regular hat and put on their creative hat and be a different version of themselves for a while. I have found it very healing and very enriching in my life.

4. Reduce screen time – drop the device habit

These days we don't need to search for reasons to look at a screen! Yes, there are benefits to modern day technology, but there are also a lot of drawbacks. The ease of access to technology (smart phones, tablets, laptops, and PCs) has completely changed our world. When I told my son about public phone boxes in the street when I grew up, and life before the internet, he looked at me oddly - his eyes glazed over: he could not even imagine ...

Fact: the average user touches their phone 2,617 times per day. Heavy users: 5,427 times per day.[13]

These stats are staggering! Hard to believe! From a purely social perspective, it is a concern to see peoples' reliance on their devices. Look around at people in the street, on the bus, train, cafes, in fact anywhere at all. They are largely communicating with others texting on their phone in short bursts rather than speaking face to face. What will happen to the art of conversation?

I don't think that I am alone with my fear that there will be far reaching social effects from texting and emailing rather than talking to people. In my family home I have banned phone use on social occasions so that we talk to each other and social skills can be learned and refined. I think that it is important to live in the moment and enjoy being present with each other.

When my son was young, he always wanted me to play with him. He kept asking if I would play his computer games with him, but I didn't want to. I prefer going outside and being active. Minecraft was a game that he was great at, and whilst I was proud of his expertise and the cleverness of the program, I had to explain that since I worked at a desk, on a computer, for most of my working day, the last thing I wanted to do was spend more time sitting down and looking at a screen! Instead I would take him to the park, and we would run around, kick balls, ride bikes, scoot, slide or swing – just as I grew up doing! I explained that it was important for both of us to be physically active and to interact with other people face to face.

---

[13]   2016: Read the whole fascinating blog by dscout: https://blog.dscout.com/mobile-touches

DONNA PORTLAND

"It has become appallingly obvious that our technology has exceeded our humanity."

unknown sage

Where does the time go? The main issue with the time spent netsurfing and playing games is that over the course of a week hours can just get squandered. When you add up the time it takes to check feeds on Facebook, Instagram, or Twitter you will start to see where your time goes and why it seems there is never enough of it.

Does reliance on technology reduce creativity? It is a common concern and has been for many years that the amount of technology we now use in everyday life, can reduce creativity, and bring about the downfall of imagination. Whilst you do see lots of images and GIFs on social media posts, it is passive, and your brain is not creating anything.

Are we just merely distracting ourselves - constantly?

What are we missing out on by embracing the phone habit?

Are we are sacrificing original thought to keep ourselves constantly entertained?

What to do instead:

Choose balance. Make a conscious effort to detach from technology from time to time and reign in the time that you pick up your device(s) to continually check things. Stop answering every single text or call. If it is really important people will leave a message on your voicemail or send you an email. It may be wise to actively think about ways in which your use of non-essential technology can be reduced. Examine your own and your family's screen-time: computer, phone, and the television. If the time-waste is a problem, you may need to set specific amount of time you are prepared to give it and keep to a plan. You will notice then that you have more time for other things. You can turn off your phone periodically and have a real life!

Slow down! Think of ways that you can reduce your obligations and/or make fewer commitments so that you have time for yourself.

Take a break. Ask yourself if you are getting enough 'down time'...? Ask if you have given yourself time to rejuvenate and re-energise?

Here are some ideas:

Read (or listen to) a book.
Listen to a variety of Podcasts.
Go for a walk.....
Take at least one day off per week.
Do something different.
Expand your horizons.
Be in the moment. Be present.

Enjoy nature! This is a marvellous 'active meditation', so get outside in the fresh air and *feel* the connection and receive inspiration.

> # IT'S ONLY BY SAYING NO THAT YOU CAN CONCENTRATE ON THE THINGS THAT REALLY MATTER.
> ### - SCOTT BELSKY -

Belsky is an American entrepreneur who is best known for co-creating the online investment portfolio platform Behance Inc. He is also an author and one of his titles "Making Ideas Happen" gives you an idea of how he's been able to achieve so much: by being able to say "No" when he needs to, so that he can get on with doing the things that are important to him to achieve his goals.

5. Learn to say "No" sometimes

Pre end of 2017, before I changed my life, I was guilty of taking on almost everything that was asked of me. I somehow felt that in order to be a good person, wife, mother, and employer I needed to be all things to all people! I honestly don't know why I operated like that. Eventually I just ran myself into the ground. I had no energy left at the end of the day. My brain would turn to mush and I would *need* a glass of wine to calm down, relax and numb myself out. Perhaps you can relate?

I often avoided social engagements because I was exhausted and because I felt that I had nothing left to give. That is so odd because I am usually keen to socialise and enjoy talking to people!

Let's be honest: who has the time to continually be doing things for others as well as all the things that you need to do for yourself. If you're a parent it's a given of course, but there needs to be a limit to how much assistance you give. If you have young children of course they are dependent but as they grow, it is important for their own development that they contribute more to their own care and also to the family collective.

You are not doing your children any favours by attending to their every need.

They may wind up 'entitled' and useless.
So back off and let them step up!
Don't encourage them become narcissistic!

Enable them instead to become independent and self-sufficient and in doing so you will have given them the greatest gift and also yourself because you will have more time for yourself if you're not constantly giving to everyone else.

If you are a leader or a boss: everyone is looking to you to solve their problems, give guidance and direction of course. It goes with the territory. You need to do the same for those you manage, as for your children: teach the people who look to you for guidance, to find their own answers. Tell them to go somewhere to think, brainstorm ideas that could address the issue, form a viable solution, and come back to discuss if they still need to. That way you will foster their independence and they will come back less often, having grown more confident in their own abilities.

If it's your partner who is always asking for your help, your time, and your resources you need to examine why and if it is balanced. Of course, there are periods in our lives when we lean on others more because our own reserves are down, but it's not healthy to conduct a relationship which is always one-sided, where one partner always demands more from the other with little reciprocation. Again, you are not doing anyone any favours - yourself or your partner - to be shouldering their burdens without a good plan to resolve the issue(s).

It seems to be human nature to want to take the easy road rather than do the work, so people will tend to try to get someone else to shoulder their load if possible, whether they are consciously aware of this or not! There are also the natural givers who want to help and are kind and generous. It is great to help people, if and when they really need the help, and wonderful if you offer to help voluntarily and for the right reasons. But don't agree to help because you want to avoid confrontation or conflict.

Don't agree to help out of a sense of guilt or because you feel obliged in some way. It is not so great when you give away your own life unconsciously and even become stressed because you are incapable of saying "No" when you need to.

It's not about saying "No" to everything either,
but you shouldn't do something that hurts you (wastes your time, drains your energy or resources, that you resent) or prevents you from attending to your own priorities.

Remember that you can only help others if you help yourself first! Remember the safety advice that the airline crew give when you fly: "in the event that the oxygen masks fall from the ceiling fit your own mask before helping others". It is so true. If you set the example, you are helping them the most.

Going forward you can consider the following before you agree to help someone:

1. **Value your time**. If saying "No" to some things allows you to say "Yes" to other things that you care about, then it is valid. The fact is that if you show others that you value your time and your priorities, they will respect you for it, and pay you the same respect.

2. **Know yourself and be clear about your own commitments**. Put *your* priorities above anything else. Act with integrity: if what someone is asking conflicts with your priorities, just politely say "No".

3. **Be discriminating**. Before you accept a request for help, think about how much time you will need. Will you have to sacrifice your time on other things in your life (personal, family, professional)?

4. **Be generous, but do not allow abuse**. If what you are being asked to do is unfair, then suggest conditions that *are* fair or simply politely say "No".

5. **Do not agree if you are undecided**. It is OK to delay your decision. Simply say that you need to think about it. If you cannot come up with solid reasons for accepting the request, then politely say "No".

6. **Do not allow others to manipulate you.** If after you decline a request for help and your relationship with that person deteriorates, it is a clear indication that it was not a sincere relationship. After all, if someone truly appreciates you, they will *never* ask you something that would harm you or deflect you from your own purpose and priorities.

7. **Don't give explanations or make up excuses**. It is *your* time. If you want to avoid the situation being repeated continually, just be honest from the start.

8. **Set the boundaries from the beginning** and express how you feel. Be polite but firm when you say "No" and try to show that you do care about people's opinions and feelings and in doing so you will gain their respect.

6. Look for Inspiration

> "You often feel tired, not because
> you've done too much,
> but because you've done too little of
> what sparks a light in you."

Dutch inspirational speaker, trainer and consultant Alexander Den Heijer is an inspirational man. He hit the nail on the head with that remark. It makes you think about what life is about without inspiration! Look around you, I imagine that it is very easy to identify people who are living without inspiration. You can usually see this on their faces.

Den Heijer also makes a very good points with these further comments:

> "When a flower doesn't bloom,
> you fix the environment in which
> it grows, not the flower."

and

> "The reason many people suffer
> is not that life is too tough;
> it's that they haven't found
> something worth living for."

DONNA PORTLAND

So clearly we need to be giving ourselves the environment that we need for our inspiration to occur and to become fruitful. It is worth finding the "something worth living for" – the inspiration!

Following on from that idea, American popular psychologist and motivational speaker Anthony Robbins reminds us to get on with it once we have decided what we are aiming for:

"Remember,
if you talk about it, it's a dream.
If you envision it, it's possible.
But if you schedule it, it's real."

So, let's get on with it!

The easy way for most of us to find some inspiration is to borrow from those who you think are inspirational. This could be people like Den Heijer or Robbins or it might be someone you already know: your friend or colleague.

It is also necessary to understand what motivates you, and the best way to do this is to get moving. Here are twelve ideas to help you find your motivation and go forward:

1. Be spontaneous.
   Use your intuition.
   Give something a go. Try things. Experiment.
   Ignore fear – do it anyway!

2. Remove yourself from distractions! At the risk of sounding like a broken record: you can step away from the phone for a while and life *will* go on!

3. Always be on the look-out for sources of inspiration wherever you are. Ideas can be found in the most unlikely places and from unlikely people – so be vigilant and keep an eye (and an ear) out for nuggets.

4. Realise that there are no stupid ideas! Don't let an idea get past without a thorough test or examination. Remember, at one stage in history light bulbs and wired telephones seemed crazy! Let go of your perfectionist tendencies. Great ideas and master plans take time and work before they reach fulfilment and clarity. So be open minded and allow ideas to flow.

5. Reading is really useful for picking up ideas. Whether this is books, mags or online, it is remarkable how much information is out there. YouTube is full of 'how to' videos

and the internet is rich with inspirational material. You do have to exercise some filtering of course. Not everything written is fact, so be discriminating, yet have an open mind to possibility!

6. Collaborate with others: Talk about your ideas. Enlist their help or collaborate on something together! We can usually achieve so much more and go forward far quicker in a team environment than we can by ourselves: greater resources, bouncing ideas, motivating, and enlightening (and fun) conversation boosts creativity. Teaming up is also a great way of making friends and extending your social circle.

7. Do not fret if you don't have a grand plan, as small ideas are golden too. Or maybe you feel that your big idea seems too complicated? It is possible to achieve pieces of the grand plan in small steps and build on your achievements in order to reach that overall goal. You may not even realise for a while where your inspiration is leading you. It is possible that your small goals can build up into something grand. I would say just go with the flow and see where you end up. (Remember to keep in tune with your intuition!)

8. When you cannot seem to get inspired and it seems like you're in a rut, let it go for a while rather than push it, but do not give up! Don't let that little negative voice inside tell you that you're just not a very motivated or talented person and just leave it there. Give yourself an opportunity to get out of your negative headspace: change what you are doing and perhaps change your environment/surroundings. Go to the gym or for a run. Intense physical activity can stimulate your mind. Come back to seeking your inspiration when you are in a more positive headspace.

9. Take a break: use your weekends to recharge and allow yourself to refocus. When you are rested you will see things in a different light.

10. Travel: it is a great way to see how other people live and explore the perspective of different cultures. Inspiration can be found by seeing new ways of doing things or discovering things you never knew existed.

11. Failure is an option! So, take the attitude that failing can provide an opportunity for learning and don't give up.

And last, but not least:

12. Meditate – *Think* – Reflect – *Be Quiet*
    Practice being quiet and give yourself time to think and reflect. Don't rush. Don't push. Just be.
    The art of meditation has been well covered in previous chapters and it is hugely important to tap into the amazing resource: of your subconscious mind. Leave out any evaluations and analysis - just let yourself come up with ideas and record them. There is plenty of time for further consideration when you're not meditating.

DONNA PORTLAND

Consider these reasons to ignore fear of failure and get on and do things anyway. We can all learn from these inspiring people.

Thomas Edison declared:

"I have not failed. I've just found 10,000 ways that won't work."

Remember that you may stumble and fall but you can get back up and get on with trying again. One failure does not mean that everything else you try will fail. If it did then we would not be enjoying light bulbs!

Robert F Kennedy said:

"Only those who dare to fail greatly can ever achieve greatly."

If no one ever dared to do something different and try something new we would never have grown as a civilisation and been able to invent the technology that changes our lives.

And my favourite insight from Friederich Nietzsche:

"A thinker sees his own actions as experiments and questions - as attempts to find out something. Success and failure are for him answers above all."

Ask questions and experiment to discover new answers! Don't be confined by fear and ego.

7. Vitality Tips to help you get to 100%

If a lack of vitality is an issue for you here is a quick list of things you could put up on your fridge to remind yourself of what you need to do.

This really worked for me. I need reminders! So, when your reserves are low you can just check the list and do something that's on it – anything – to help you take a positive step forward when you're lacking motivation.

Go to bed 30 minutes earlier than usual. Aim for 8 hours of sleep each night. Calm your mind and eyes – avoid texting, watching TV or exercise before bed.

Get up 30 - 60 minutes earlier. Use the time to think and set your plans for the day or to exercise or meditate.

Take some quiet time during the day - try at least 15 minutes to sit quietly and relax or meditate. Get extra value by doing it outside in the fresh air and sunlight.

Exercise - find a form that you are excited to do – and commit to it on a regular basis. When you walk, focus on your breathing, not your cell phone.

Drink 2-3 litres of pure water daily.

Eat high water content vegetables making the ratio 70% of what is on your plate. Alkalinize your diet.

Do a cleanse or detox to jump start you towards a change.

Eliminate toxic (inflammatory) foods, colourings, artificial flavourings, preservatives, fillers, and allergens from your diet.

Eliminate Sugar from your diet. Keep reducing and reducing until you get used to not having sugar. This will mean saying "NO" to confectionary, added sugar in tea and coffee, biscuits, cake, commercial breakfast cereals and processed foods.

Be present with people and express yourself authentically and tell those you love and value how you feel. Put away your phone when you're in the company of people.

Dance to music or just allow yourself to be fully absorbed in music for at least 15 - 30 minutes.

Look for opportunities to be creative. Seek and you will find!

Give yourself the healthcare treatments that you need: massage, reiki, reflexology, chiropractic, acupuncture, ear candling, dental, podiatry, optometry, skin cancer checks, mammograms, pap smears, prostate checks, blood tests, hair analysis for heavy metals, et al.

Take Action: List the important and immediate changes that you would like to achieve. Make those goals your priority. Even if you make only one change a week, you will reach four changes in a month and they will become part of your life. If you do more, you will get there sooner!

Congratulations – you have finished part 1 – the physical aspects of your daily habits.

PART 2

The second part of this book is about positive habits for your mind. The feeling of being energetic is both physical and mental. We look at the mental aspects and positive habits that can positively change your life.

CHAPTER 8
AN ATTITUDE OF GRATITUDE

Gratitude is the first chapter of Part 2 of this book for a very good reason. Much has been written about gratitude because it is pivotal to feeling satisfied and happy with your life.

Adopting an attitude of gratitude means making it a habit to express thankfulness and appreciation in all parts of your life, <u>on a regular basis</u>, for the big and small things alike.

The idea is to *always* be grateful and then you will experience more joy in your life. It works.

I first became attracted to this idea when I discovered this beautifully expressed quote from Melody Beattie:

"Gratitude unlocks the fullness of life.
It turns what we have into enough, and more.
It turns denial into acceptance,
chaos to order, confusion to clarity.
It can turn a meal into a feast,
a house into a home, a stranger into a friend." [14]

I have attended several talks given by Dr John Demartini [15] who says that gratitude is the key or gateway of the heart and love. He is a learned man and a fascinating speaker. It has meant a lot to me to discover that by focusing on the feeling of gratitude it inspires enthusiasm and links to your values.

---

[14] https://melodybeattie.com/books/gratitude-inspirations-melody-beattie/
[15] https://drdemartini.com/

I also discovered a powerful book written by Lewis Howes entitled "Attitude of Gratitude" and the simple truth of it really struck me:

> ## "If you concentrate on what you have,
> ### *you'll always have more.*
>
> ## If you concentrate on what you don't have,
> ### *you'll never have enough."*

I admit that I previously fell into the second category. My mother had always implied that scarcity was the reality. She would not waste a single thing. She didn't like to spend money either. I grew up with a mindset of lack. After my father's departure and their subsequent divorce Mum did her best to provide materially and saw that my siblings and I were well-educated and well-cared for, and that we had what we needed, but there were no frills in our existence. Life always seemed like there was never quite enough of anything - except problems and issues... I wanted to experience the *feeling* of "always having more" instead.

I wanted to know how to change this mindset and change my life! It was time to explore and this meant a lot of reading and learning how to truly listen.

Lewis Howes' book is a *must read*. He created a 'menu of tactics' to help people develop a grateful mindset. Here is a list of his suggestions that really work for me and it is my hope that they will work for you too.

Wake up every day and express to **yourself** what you are grateful for

Tell **whoever you are with at the end of the day** the three things you are most grateful for

Tell **whoever you are with right now** (significant other, friend, family member, ...) the three things that you are most grateful for in this moment

Start a **gratitude journal** - express gratitude in this journal every night by noting the things that you are thankful for, proud of, and excited about

Acknowledge yourself for what you have done and accomplished in the last day/week/month/year. Instead of comparing yourself to others, give yourself credit for the big and small things you have been doing!

DONNA PORTLAND

Acknowledge other people and thank them for inspiring/helping/supporting you – oftentimes people wait their whole lives to be acknowledged (and yet it happens far too infrequently)!

I found this to be marvellous advice and put into practice the things he suggests. At one point on my social media profile every day I would think up and post "Three things I am grateful for today". The result was amazing. You experience the things you think about and I feel grateful and plentiful now. In the beginning this practice was really just for me to be mindful but I have found that it affected others in a positive way also. These days I post less often but I still actively think of the things that I am grateful for each day.

Howes suggests that if the gratitude process is hard to get started, you can begin by asking yourself, "What *could* I be grateful for?", and see if the ideas start to flow. I noticed that Anthony Robbins recommends this same mindset/habit in his book, "Awaken the Giant Within". I have included this book in a suggested reading list about Gratitude at the end of this chapter. I also discovered many excellent gratitude meditations on YouTube, from which I found tremendous value.

Of course, every day will not be perfect, but when you focus on what you are grateful for the feelings of anger and negativity tend to wash away.

On my quest for knowledge about how to change the way I experienced my reality, apart from the need to embrace gratitude I came across the concept of the "Law of Attraction" which explains how the way you think creates your reality. I feel that the two ideas are interlinked.

Here are the basic ideas behind the "Law of Attraction" concept:

You are the creator of your own reality.

What we think, we create, what we feel, we attract, what we imagine, we become.

You get in life what you have the COURAGE to ask for.

If you can imagine it in your mind, you can experience it in your REALITY.

There is nothing you can *not* have.
There are no limitations.

All abundance starts first in the mind.

Just CREATE, do not PROCRASTINATE.

The entire universe is working in your favour!

Anthony Robbins[16] expresses this same idea as
"Life is happening <u>for</u> me"
(as opposed to "Life is happening <u>to</u> me!")

If you can BELIEVE it, you can ACHIEVE it.

Dr Wayne Dyer[17] said something very similar in his
book: "You'll see it when you believe it!"

**"The Law of Attraction is ALWAYS working,
whether you believe it is or not".**

"What would you do if you could create anything
on earth? And why are you waiting?"

**"It is unlimited what the universe can bring,
when you understand the great secret,
that thoughts become things."**

"Today, I EXPECT and BELIEVE in miracles."

- Fearless Soul [18]

**The law of attraction is ALWAYS responding
to your vibration.
It doesn't care for your belief in or against it,
it is only responding to what you are putting out.**

---

16 https://www.tonyrobbins.com/mind-meaning/life-is-happening-for-me/
17 https://www.drwaynedyer.com/
18 https://iamfearlesssoul.com/

*"See yourself living in abundance
and you will attract it.
It always works, it works every time,
with every person"*

**"Thoughts become things.
If you see it in your mind you will hold it in your hand"**

- Bob Proctor [19]

"The better you FEEL, the more you ALLOW."

"You have the ability to quickly change your patterns of
thought, and eventually your life experience."

- Abraham Hicks [20]

Although you intuitively know that the idea of gratitude being good for your health and well-being is on point, it is always comforting to know that there is science behind the claims. Paul Mills, a Professor of Family Medicine and Public Health at the University of California San Diego School of Medicine, conducted studies that looked at the role of gratitude on heart health[21]. Note that Dr Deepak Chopra was amongst the ten researchers on that study.

Mills' findings, among other things, were that participants who kept a journal most days of the week, writing about 2-3 things they were grateful for (everything from appreciating their children to travel and good food), had reduced levels of inflammation and improved heart rhythm compared to people who did not write in a journal. And the journal-keepers also showed a decreased risk of heart disease after only two months of this new routine.

And in addition to improving mood, studies showed that feeling and expressing gratitude lead to better physical health as well.

To summarise:

A regular practice of gratitude, or 'attitude of gratitude' if you prefer, can enhance your life in a multitude of ways:

- Enhanced well-being and satisfaction with life

---

19 https://www.proctorgallagherinstitute.com/
20 https://www.abraham-hicks.com/
21 Source: https://www.ncbi.nlm.nih.gov/pmc/articles/PMC4507265/

- Higher quality relationships with loved ones
- Better physical health
- Improving mood
- Reduction in symptoms of depression.

Gratitude is a huge subject which has been extensively written about, so I feel that it is best to give you a powerful reading list than try to summarise all of it here. Choose whichever one(s) you want or find your own with a search of the internet - whatever you choose will be the right thing to read. Remember that when the student is ready, the teacher appears!

"Attitude of Gratitude" (2016) by Lewis Howes

> Imagine feeling proud, thankful, and joyful on an ongoing basis, not only during the holiday season! As Howes simply says, "*Life is better if you develop an attitude of gratitude.*" In his inspirational book he explains what that means and how we can cultivate a grateful mindset and make it a habit to express thankfulness and appreciation in all parts of your life, on a regular basis, for both the big and small things alike. Just start "concentrating on what you have, you'll always have more".

"The Little Book of Gratitude: Create a Life of Happiness and Wellbeing by Giving Thanks" (2016) by Robert A. Emmons

> This author has written many books on gratitude, but this is the simplest. He describes how we can improve our health and wellbeing, enhance our relationships, encourage healthy sleep, and heighten feelings of connectedness, increase happiness, and encourage greater joy, love, peace, and optimism into our lives. This wonderful book discusses the benefits of gratitude and teaches easy techniques to foster gratitude every day through easy practices such as keeping a daily gratitude journal, writing letters of thanks, and meditating on the good already present in our lives.

Other Gratitude books by Emmons (and colleagues):

> **"Words of Gratitude for Mind, Body, and Soul"** by R. Emmons and Joanna Hill

> **"The Psychology of Gratitude"** by R. Emmons and Michael McCullough

> **"Thanks! How the New Science of Gratitude Can Make You Happier"** by R Emmons

"Gratitude" (2015) by Oliver Sacks – A Short Summary

People don't usually associate Oliver Sacks with this genre as he was the respected neurologist who wrote the famous book "The Man Who Mistook His Wife for a Hat" (1985) which really got him noticed, along with many other essays and books.

After he'd been diagnosed with terminal cancer in January 2015 he wrote a stirring and emotional essay in The New York Times and shared these words: *"I cannot pretend I am without fear. But my predominant feeling is one of gratitude. I have loved and been loved. I have been given much and I have given something in return. Above all, I have been a sentient being, a thinking animal, on this beautiful planet, and that in itself has been an enormous privilege and adventure."*.

This is the essence of his final book Gratitude - an ode to life, to love, to mortality, and to the unique pleasures and challenges that accompany being human.

"A Simple Act of Gratitude: How Learning to Say Thank You Changed My Life" (2011) by John Kralik

During a particularly difficult time in his life, Kralik had an epiphany - perhaps he would find life more manageable if he focused on what he *did* have rather than what he didn't have!

This touching memoir will change you, as the author describes how he went from an all-time low to a happy and flourishing life through the simple act of writing thank-you notes. He began his gratitude journey by setting a goal for himself: over a year to write 365 handwritten thank-you notes, one each day. As he did so, he noticed profound changes occurring in his life. This book outlines a roadmap for anyone wanting to make similar changes in their life.

"The Gratitude Diaries: How a Year Looking on the Bright Side Can Transform Your Life" (2015) by Janice Kaplan

The author details her personal journey and resolve to become more grateful and optimistic. She weaves academic research and evidence-based findings in with her own personal journey to present you with an excellent reason to give gratitude a shot. The tone of the book is informal and accessible, so an excellent choice for the more casual reader interested in gratitude, and it presents a message that everyone can benefit from receiving.

"Everyday Gratitude: Inspiration for Living Life as a Gift" (2018) by A Network for Grateful Living (a global organization offering online and community-based educational programs and practices that inspire and guide a commitment to grateful living and catalyse the transformative power of personal and societal responsibility. gratefulness.org) introduction by Kristi Nelson.

This book is a collection of quotes and reflections and inspiration from well-known minds, which aim to help you discover that the roots of happiness lie in gratefulness.

"Stop-Look-Go: A Grateful Practice Workbook and Gratitude Journal" (2016) produced and edited by Gary Fiedel and Karie Jacobson

Using the STOP, LOOK, GO technique gratefully borrowed from Brother David Steindl-Rast, this workbook and journal provides the building blocks to a grateful life so that you can experience the joy of grateful living through practical instructions, exercises and essays. The book offers 32 exercises that explore all aspects of grateful living: from the foundations of gratefulness to being grateful in hard times.

"May Cause Happiness: A Gratitude Journal" (2018) by Br. David Steindl-Rast, OSB

The visually inspiring pages in Brother David's journal invite us to spark our own thankfulness when feeling weary or numb, transform our "dismissible" moments into fresh delights, dance with both the light and dark we encounter, and merge with the stream of the natural world.

He has shared the blessings of the thankful heart with millions via his books and appearances and invites us to find greater depth and joy amid our daily challenges and burdens. "It is not happiness that makes us grateful, but gratefulness that makes us happy."

"Awaken the Giant Within" (2001) by Anthony Robbins

You could read any of Robbins' books as they all provide strategies to change the way you think so you can enjoy a more positive outlook and fulfilling life. In all his education he focusses on gratitude and his ideas are easy to implement. You will always find great positive insights for changing your mindset!

The primary question Robbins asks is 'Are you in charge of your life?' Or are you being swept away by things that are seemingly out of your control? He shows you how to take immediate control of your mental, emotional, physical, and financial destiny.

CHAPTER 9
JOURNALING & DREAMING

During my most troubling times when my mind was spinning with fear, indecision, pain, hurt, grief, and anger I just wanted peace. I would have given anything for a quiet mind. I wanted to get rid of the random thoughts that swirled around my brain. I wanted to get them out of my head. *I* wanted to control what I thought about. ...not too much to ask right?!! I am sure you know what I mean. Everyone seems to suffer from unwanted, persistent thoughts bombarding their mind from time to time!

I wasn't doing so well at meditation in the beginning - that took a while to master and I am still working on it! The practice that helped me the most with clearing my mind was journaling. For me it is a form of meditation to write, doodle, draw and paint and so I indulged in this pastime to find some peace.

It is amazing where the pearls of wisdom can come from in life. I met a sage lady, manager of a women's retreat in Bali where I stayed in bliss for two weeks. We discussed my dilemma (of those annoying circular thoughts) and she suggested I read a book entitled "The Artist's Way: A spiritual Path to Higher Creativity" by Julia Cameron. It is a fascinating book that all artists - amateur or professional - would do well to read, as it deals very well with the touchy subject of 'creative block'.

In order to clear your mind each day Cameron's suggestion is to journal. What this means is that you sit down with your morning beverage soon after waking and write it down! Fill at least three sheets of paper with your thoughts and literally empty your brain out onto the pages! **I found this to be 100% effective.**

I call this process "Download Journaling" because that's how it felt. I'd just scrawl down every thought onto the page and once it was 'downloaded' it was gone, and I'd move onto the next one, write that down and move on to the next, and so on. The thing I found quite amazing was the sheer *amount* of thoughts that I had previously allowed to swirl endlessly, which caused me a good deal of stress. Now, at last, I could get rid of them onto the page and my mind was very happy with that. I was making space for the thoughts I actually wanted to think! It was a form of housekeeping for my brain.

Instructions for the simple download journaling method:

- Wake up, deep breathe x 5, grab your pen and paper and sit down with a cup of tea, hot water with lemon, or whatever beverage you fancy.

- You can even walk if you want to, but you will need to bring a clipboard with your pages and pen and stop whenever there is a thought to purge! (Don't forget to bring water with you, as it is always a great idea to keep hydrated.)

- Write down whatever comes into your mind. Once you have written it down, move on to the next thought and keep going.

- The aim is not to re-read these writings, although you can if you want to. Sometimes I would asterisk things that I didn't want to forget, i.e. appointments, important 'to do' list items, etc.

- Stop when you have run out of circular thoughts or managed to fill three pages. If you've still got more to write after three pages, then keep going until you run out.

- You will feel very peaceful once you have emptied your head. Enjoy it.

The reason that I like this kind of journaling is that there is absolutely no stress in filling your pages. You are not aiming for literary brilliance or to be creative. This is not to show someone else. The benefit is for you alone and success lies in the removal of stress from your mind.

Then there is Journaling in the general sense which is more of a free form of writing - less about recording events, more about externalising feelings, being reflective and going deeper into your thoughts. This is more of a 'Phase 2', after you have conquered the crazy thoughts state of mind that were first described.

Writing in a paper journal by hand helps you to slow down and allows you to really think. There are a number of excellent benefits of journaling.

1. **You will improve as a writer** if this is your aim. Practice makes perfect! Even if you're not aiming to be a writer as a profession, there are loads of reasons and professions where skill at writing is very useful. If you get into the habit of putting thoughts into words, practising expression, and exploring motivations it will become easy for you. You will be in excellent company too, as many great writers have advocated the value of keeping a journal.

2. **You will keep focussed**. By dedicating a few minutes each day to honour yourself, your thoughts and your feelings instead of only paying attention to all the usual

things (work, study, children, family obligations, domestics, etcetera), journaling can help remind you who you are, what you want and whether you're living your life as the kind of person you want to be. It is also a great chance to practice being grateful. It can be an opportunity to remind yourself how good your life really is, instead of paying attention to the distractions or allowing the little things to get you down.

3. **Your health could improve.** Scientists have even found that the act of journaling can boost your immunity. A ground-breaking study published in the Journal of the American Medical Association (Vol. 281, No. 14) asked patients with asthma and patients with rheumatoid arthritis to write for twenty minutes on three consecutive days about the most stressful event of their lives and the rest about the emotionally neutral subject of their daily plans. Four months after the writing exercise, 70 patients in the stressful-writing group showed improvement on objective, clinical evaluations compared with 37 of the control patients.

In a more recent study at the University of Auckland (NZ), researchers found a similar pattern among HIV/AIDS patients. The researchers asked 37 patients in four 30-minute sessions to write about negative life experiences or about their daily schedules. The patients who wrote about life experiences measured higher on immune functioning immediately after. So, it seems that by writing, you put some structure and organisation to your anxious feelings which helps you to get past them.

4. **Preserve your great ideas.** Have you ever noticed when you have a fabulous idea and tell your brain to remember it, because you didn't have a pen at the time of having the thought, and later when you try to remember the epiphany it's evaporated into thin air? It is completely gone from your consciousness ... Your pen can record all your amazing ideas. Let them flow, write them down. The act of exploring them can give them shape and bring them to life! So, your journal can become an incubator for ideas and a place to express your dreams. You can later work through and make plans and spend time developing those ideas and dreams. Most of all you can capture those fleeting thoughts to revisit later and fully consider without fear of losing them.

5. **Become aware of your dreams!** It could be quite fascinating to bring your dreams (or thoughts that occupy your mind whilst you sleep) into your consciousness. The exact purpose of dreaming isn't known, but it's thought to help you to process your emotions. Events from the day often invade your thoughts during sleep, and people suffering from stress or anxiety are more likely to have frightening dreams. Dreams can be experienced in all stages of sleep but usually are most vivid in REM sleep. Some people dream in colour, while others only recall dreams in black and white. Remember your dreams by writing them down. It is very hard, nigh impossible, to

remember your dreams if you don't write them down as soon as you wake. They will disappear!

That is your actual dreams. But what about your day-dreams - your wish-list? Write down your goals and all the things you would like to accomplish. These can be listed and thought about and acted upon.

6. **Enjoy "me time".** It is great to have some time when you are alone with your thoughts and feelings. You can be creative or plan your day without interruption or distraction. In your journal you do not just express yourself more openly than you can to others; you create yourself.

How to start journaling?

Your attitude needs to be: "I can do this, but I mustn't make it too intimidating" and it should be easy to accomplish.

1. **Use paper, not a computer** as you will find the experience much more creative. The pace of writing and drawing is slower, and your brain operates differently giving you more time for thought to drift in. Pause, take your time, and enjoy the difference.

2. **Collect for your precious journal.** Buy a journal that inspires you to open it. Don't worry about spoiling it. It's yours and it's perfect for its purpose. Collect special things to put into it and create an interesting piece.

3. **Be free:** use different materials, make a mess, experiment, don't obsess about the outcome – just do it.

4. **Time yourself.** Give yourself X minutes maximum per day to make your mark. You choose how much time: from 10 - 30 mins depending on what else you have to accomplish in the day. Let yourself off the hook if you just cannot get to it one day - and aim for a longer stint the following day.

5. **Don't fear the blank page.** You do not need to create a masterpiece; avoid overwhelm by just writing or drawing something in the journal every day to get into the swing of it. As you begin to see the pages fill up with images and ideas, you will get the sense that you're creating something.

6. **Take a chance** – be random. Just try things.

DONNA PORTLAND

Plan your Day

This will set you up for a productive day with less stress than if you just fly out the door in a mad rush. It may only take 10-15 minutes. The more practise you get the more efficient you will become.

1. Go to the bathroom, then get your cup of tea (or glass of water).
2. Set aside some time to sit in peace while you think.
3. Breathe deeply.
4. Best to be alone in silence.
5. Be certain about your aim and priorities.
6. Best to use a computer this time so that you can edit and rearrange priorities.

Suggested reading: "The Artist's Way: A spiritual Path to Higher Creativity" by Julia Cameron.

CHAPTER 10

MIND MASTERY

This chapter is about taking control. Instead of feeling, as so many people do, that they are having to roll with the punches - at the mercy of things that happen in their lives, you *can* learn to direct your thoughts, and become aware of the 'unconscious' things that you do that negatively affect your experience and choose to exercise different patterns.

"The biggest wall you have to climb is the one you build in your own mind:

Never let your mind talk you out of your dreams, trick you into giving up.

Never let your mind become the greatest obstacle to success.

Get your mind on the right track, the rest will follow."

Roy T. Bennett [22]

I also read an excellent book written by Napoleon Hill [23] (1937), "Think and Grow Rich" where he had spent some 25 years studying the methods and thinking of a wide variety

---

[22] Roy T. Bennett is the author of The Light in the Heart. He loves sharing positive thoughts and creative insight that has helped countless people to live a successful and fulfilling life. https://thelightintheheart.wordpress.com/author/roytbennett/

[23] https://www.naphill.org/ The motto of the Napoleon Hill Foundation is, "Making the world a better place in which to live." If you believe that life has purpose or meaning, then you can leave a legacy that helps make the world a better place. The decisions that you make - or do not make - will help determine the type of legacy you leave behind. Whether you are part of the solutions to the cries for help or part of the problems that confront the human race will be a result of your actions on a daily basis.

of successful people who had mastered their thinking and gained pin-point focus. What an enlightened idea! No wonder it became an all-time bestseller and still is, despite being written some 80-odd years ago. I recommend that you read it as the content is every bit as valid today as when the book was first written. Obviously, technology has changed but the habits and methods of successful people have remained the same.

The main message from all my study on this subject is that to gain mastery of your mind you *primarily* need to **keep focussed**.

Do these six things: (elaboration on these key points follows)

1. Know precisely what you want to achieve and maintain focus.

2. Be single minded. When you catch yourself straying - pull yourself back to where you need to be focussed.

3. Focus on the priority.

4. Choose what *you* allow to influence you.

5. Stay present in the moment.

6. Let things go... FORGIVE. Let go of negativity... be POSITIVE.

Now for the commentary:

Point 1: Know precisely what you want to achieve and maintain focus.

Napoleon Hill also said:

> **"No one may achieve success without first knowing precisely what he wants.**
>
> **Study any person who is known to be a permanent success and you will find that he has a Definite Major Goal; he has a plan for the attainment of this goal; he devotes the major portion of his thoughts and his efforts to the attainment of this purpose."**

And further:

> **"You either control your mind,**
> **or it controls you."**

We have become lazy in controlling our minds - we let rampant negative thoughts run riot sometimes. Enough! This was happening to me, so I *decided* I needed to change. I had to actively choose to think differently.

When you catch yourself worrying and thinking excessively (unnecessarily or for a reason), you can *decide* to deal with it then and there, or park it for now (to be dealt with later). When you need a distraction, you can choose, as I did, to go for a walk to clear your head. The fresh air and exercise will also assist your body (and mind) on a physical level.

When you realise that you've taken your eye off the ball, *decide* to re-focus.

When you discover yourself jumping to conclusions with insufficient evidence to support the story you are telling yourself, don't fall into the trap. Think well and take a 'scientific' approach, looking for evidence before reaching judgement.

Point 2: Be single minded. Being single-minded and disciplined is clearly necessary if you wish to attain your goals and live your purpose. Whenever you stray from your purpose you waste your time and energy. When you suspect you've gotten off track and you catch yourself straying, ask yourself: *"What do I need to do to regain focus and get back on track?"* Then pull yourself back to where you need to be focussed. Here is a practical example: You can actively change how you look at something that you are struggling to control. For example, if you really crave pasta but you are trying to eat less carbohydrates in your new healthy diet regime, try imagining those carbs as toxic. See the pasta as having changed its properties and imagine the 'poison' infecting your intestines, organs, and your cells. You won't want to eat that pasta when you get those mental images! If you can mentally turn desirable things (like chocolate and wine etc.) into less desirable things it will assist you to exercise your self-control to avoid eating that pasta (chocolate or wine).

Point 3: Focus on the priority. This means filling your day with high-priority actions that inspire you – or it will fill up with rubbish (low priority stuff) that distracts you.

When you have made a solid plan, you can see it through. Whenever distractions get in the way, you can take stock, look at things logically and reasonably, and decide where the priority lies. Then it is possible to re-focus on your priority to keep on track.

Point 4: Choose what *you* allow to influence you and STOP WHINING: *you* are in control.

Learn to balance perceptions from the inside and *decide* what influences you want to expose yourself to. It's your choice what you allow to influence you: is it a steady flow of mindless television shows or head-banging music, advertisements, social media or nay-sayer people who give their opinions regardless of whether they know anything about the subject or not?

If you want to master your own mind you need to build up your belief in *yourself* as the person you listen to the most! Positive self-talk is paramount and very effective in changing your expectations and your outcomes. It is only possible to change things in your reality if you can change your mindset, think positively and truly believe that you can achieve that success. Easy right? OK – it takes time but if you start facing your problems/goals, tackling them and overcoming them, one by one, you'll notice how much progress you've made, and you'll see how far you've come and how much you've grown.

It is your own 'self-talk' that will make the biggest difference to your experience of success. Keep telling yourself that you will succeed and exercise control of your mind over and over again.

Rather than catastrophising, encourage optimism - in your own mind - about as many things as you can: your abilities, significant people in your life, people in general, your boss, life in general, the economy, the environment, random happenings, etc. etc.

Point 5: Stay present in the moment. Staying present means maintaining your focus on whatever is happening right now. So, if you are spending time with your children (or partner) don't be off somewhere else in your head planning things for next week or thinking about problems at work. You'll miss the interaction and probably half your life, according to studies by Harvard University[24] that claim "About 47% of waking hours is spent thinking about what *isn't* going on" ... and this mind-wandering typically makes people unhappy. That is a shocking and sad statistic. It seems that in the midst of all the multitasking we do, we miss emotional connections and we are aware of this and feel guilty as well.

You *can* choose to slow time down by focussing on the now. You will be able to empathise more and reduce the amount of stress and overwhelm you feel. You will improve your social skills and strengthen your connections with people who will respond positively to the authenticity they will feel from you. When you are present your head is no longer filled with future scenarios: "what will they think if I do this?" or with past scenarios "what did he mean when he said that?". You let go of your self-consciousness. You are just here, with your attention focused outward towards the person you're interacting with you just let things flow out of you. They will also feel that you are truly listening as it will show up in your general vibe and body language.

Other 'side effects' of being present are stress release, less worrying and overthinking, more openness, more appreciation of the world, improved creativity, and more playfulness.

---

[24] Read the whole article: https://news.harvard.edu/gazette/story/2010/11/wandering-mind-not-a-happy-mind/

Q: How do you get there? to 'presence'

A: Focus on your breath, focus on what is right in front of you, and pick up on the vibe you get from 'present' people. If you don't know anyone like that you could try listening to Eckhart Tolle[25]. He is a spiritual teacher who is endorsed by many high-profile people. I suggest you read his books and listen to his recordings.

The other important message here is: **Let go of the past!** Realise that there is a difference to 'what happened' as opposed to the story that you told yourself about what happened.... when you were five! Many people use negative experiences and occurrences from their childhood or some incident in the past to overgeneralise about (or predict) how the future will be. They use these negative past experiences as excuses for why they are not successful, or not happy, or why life isn't fair, and it is not their fault ... etc. etc. ad nauseum. It is a complete waste of your life to allow the past to exert an effect on your future.

> **WAKE UP: you can change your life going forward.**
> **You just need to <u>decide</u> to do it.**
> **Your future starts now.**
> **The past has no bearing on the future -** *unless you allow it.*

Point 6: Let things go! FORGIVE. Let go of negativity.

Realise that the story - the meaning - that you gave things that happened in your life, is just that: a story! Don't let that story continue to determine how you feel and behave for the rest of your life. Let it go.

If you are having trouble letting go perhaps the interesting solution proposed by Ajahn Brahm, a Caucasian Buddhist monk, will help. It is called "Four Ways of Letting Go"[26] and available on YouTube (with over 1.7 million views)!

The basic ideas are, in essence:

1. Throw away the things you've been carrying; that are heavy and imprisoning you.

   - Let go of the past, don't keep it.
   - Let go of the future - you can't change or influence it - so stop worrying about it.
   - Throw away all the fault-finding and complaining that you are doing: let go of negativity!
   - Stop overthinking because this prevents you from enjoying life. Focus on the positive feeling of life.

---

[25] https://www.eckharttolle.com/
[26] https://www.youtube.com/watch?v=USC5MJVZLy8&t=1827s

DONNA PORTLAND

2. There is freedom for you to change your attitude to contentment. Ask for what you want, but don't demand it.

3. Give and expect nothing in return. Focus on your love, even if you do not get everything you want. Expect nothing but be ready for anything.

4. Enjoy the moment – enjoy now. Cultivate a 'teflon mind': let go and enjoy this moment and then the next, not allowing the last moment to affect the next one! Accept whatever happens.

Contemplate these three powerful quotes by famous sages from history. Absorb their intended meaning. Be with these ideas for a while and remember them!

"The secret of health for both mind and body is not to mourn for the past, nor to worry about the future, but to live the present moment wisely and earnestly."

Buddha

"There is only one time that is important – NOW! It is the most important time because it is the only time that we have any power."

Leo Tolstoy

The weak can never forgive.
Forgiveness is the attribute of the strong.

Mahatma Gandhi.

It takes a lot of time and space in your head to continue to harbour negativity and ill will towards those that have hurt you or let you down, and the only person it affects is you! Remembering and reliving the pain does not serve you. When you learn how to let go of negativity from the past, you can start to focus more on the present moment and worry less about things that you cannot control, for example your past or the future.

Here is a personal share that relates to this point: I broke my arm in August 2019. It was an accident that could have been prevented. There are two ways you can react to this sort of thing: get annoyed and bothered, whinge and complain about the pain, the inconvenience, the expense, etc. etc. Or you can choose to look for the gift. This sounds a bit odd I know, but there is always something to learn from things that happen - if you look. To cut a long story short, I now realise that I could have avoided this accident if I had maintained my focus and not lost it at the wrong moment. I could have prevented my hand from contacting the hard surface at high velocity, shattering my distal radius! The lesson was "keep your eye on the ball" so to speak! STAY FOCUSSED. It was a hard way to learn a lesson but a very valuable lesson all the same.

On the upside I discovered how amazingly competent I am one-armed - as it was my non-dominant arm that I was relying on! I managed admirably: I adapted, I got on with things and I refused to succumb to negativity about it. Instead I celebrated the competent and friendly medical staff on the journey (through accident centre, to the Xray staff, to the orthopaedic surgeon, to the theatre staff and finally the physiotherapist). I also appreciated the understanding and kindness of strangers, as well as my tenacity in keeping life going as usual despite the changes to my ability and options.

Interestingly there was a further gift for me. I literally 'lost my grip' for a while. I was ruminating on this and asked myself whether I *needed* to lose my grip on anything in my life, and it turned out that I did. There was one person in my life who I had held a grudge against for 15-years ... It was time to let that go! So, I contacted her to arrange a meeting. To be honest I didn't know what I would say. In my mind she had *seriously* mucked up all those years ago for me to have gone to the lengths of banishing her! When I did catch up a few weeks later and I mentioned that I was letting it go, she spontaneously hugged me. It felt good to get rid of the negativity that I had held onto for so long.

Letting go needs to happen regardless of whether the person ends up knowing you have let it go or not. Obviously if the person you have held a grudge against has passed away or is not contactable, then you won't be able to tell them. However, you can still let go in your mind and emotions and move on.

We cannot live in the present if we cling to the past. Let go and create space for positive thoughts and experiences.

How can I let go?

Here are some easy ideas.

1. **Let go of negative language** and drop the "I hate ..." and the "I'm sick and tired of ..." Actively stop yourself from going there. These mantras do *not* help. Catch yourself when you do it and be mindful. It gets easier to make this a permanent change when you become aware that you are doing it!

2. **Forgive**: This benefits you by setting you free from the pain. It simply means releasing the negative energy that you have been holding on to. Forgiveness is a choice between remaining stuck in the past and moving ahead toward a fulfilling life and the experience of an 'easy' mind.

   Remember that the past is gone. You don't have to keep revisiting it!

   Say these positive and empowering statements to yourself:

   • I live only in the present.
   • I forgive myself for being imperfect like everyone else. It is a human condition!
   • I forgive everyone from my life in the past.
   • I love myself now and into the future.
   • I move beyond forgiveness to understanding and I have compassion and kindness for all.
   • I am a forgiving, loving, gentle and kind soul.

   If forgiveness is a big issue for you, consider Hypnosis to assist. There are also some excellent visualisations that can help to get over the forgiveness hurdle. In the 'further reading' section at the end of this chapter there are also some excellent and in-depth books specifically on this subject.

3. **Journaling:** I mentioned this in a previous chapter, so please refer to that section for a fuller explanation, however, to cover it briefly here: by writing about your thoughts and feelings it can bring some much-needed clarity. This can then provide a sense of closure that facilitates the process of moving on.

4. **Learn your lessons:** Look for the learnings in whatever has happened in the past. What was the message? Take that message and move on.

5. **Affirmations**: Affirm to yourself useful things that resonate. Above examples were centred on Forgiveness. Here is a great one for being positive: *"I am in charge of how I feel and today I am choosing happiness"* and here is another *"I have limitless potential to succeed and I can conquer any challenge"*. If you do an internet search for

DONNA PORTLAND

affirmation ideas, you will find them on every subject. Sort through and customise them for yourself and most meaningful to your situation.

6. **Be Proactive - Be Positive.** Things will not change unless *you* make it happen. Brainstorm ideas that will put you into a positive frame of mind. This could include: talking to a good friend, socialising with like-minded and positive people - not succumbing to whingeing, doing one of your favourite hobbies or pastimes, doing something kind and helpful for someone else, meditating on the positive things in your life, volunteering, watching an upbeat movie or a comedy, getting out into the fresh air, exercising, and so on.

Suggested reading:

"The Power of NOW" and "Stillness Speaks" by Eckhart Tolle

"Think and Grow Rich" by Napoleon Hill

Search the internet for affirmations that target your area of interest and reword them, as necessary.

CHAPTER 11

MANAGE YOUR TIME - SPEND IT WISELY

Are you caught in a time trap? This is an important question that we all need to ask ourselves and answer honestly.

This was a huge problem for me. I had not realised how many time-sapping activities were going on in my life until I stopped long enough to take a good look and evaluate.

Where did all my time go? and why was there never enough time for me? I needed to analyse, take off the blinkers and be honest. I needed to be clear about my priorities, then rearrange them. It is essential to do this every few months especially as priorities can and do change over time.

I needed to apportion my time according to my highest priority and delegate the less important tasks to others if I wanted to achieve the important things.

Getting organised and planning my time would ensure that I achieved balance in my life and gave myself sufficient 'me time' when I was not working. This means time for relaxation, exercise, personal 'alone time' as well as 'family time'.

It may sound very structured to plan one's life to this extent, but it is only necessary in the beginning until you establish a more satisfying habit. Then it's easy to do ongoing. It just rolls out. This is the beauty of creating habits - especially positive ones!

Focus on your Work/Life balance:

Consider this:

> What we think about is what we **FIND** time for.
>
> What we care about is what we **MAKE** time for.
>
> What we love we will **INVEST** time in.
>
> We always find time, make time and invest time in *what matters to us.*
>
> And we **SAVE** time if we discard the things just fill time...*(like watching TV, for example)*
>
> Where we **SPEND** our time will determine the quality of our lives.
>
> And we cannot expect to change that which we give **NO** time for.

Please re-read the words in the box above about your focus on work/life balance, and consider,

What do *you* mostly think about?

Care about?

Love?

and invest your time in?

There is a Worksheet/Exercise at the end of this chapter where you will be encouraged to take a careful look. We will go to the extent of estimating the time you spend doing the various things you do, so that you can notice where it may be skewed. This reveals the truth about your work/life balance, your interests, and what matters to you most: your priorities! It may be confronting. It will be a useful exercise as you will discover if you need to make changes to bring things back into balance.

Are you giving enough time to achieving quality time for family? for relaxation and fun?

Remember that thought provoking epigram by Confucius:

"We all have two lives. The second one begins when we realise that we only have one."

This is an amazing gift when you think about it. You have an opportunity to realise the truth of this and do something about it.

No one gets to their deathbed and says, *"I wish I'd worked more! ... and spent less time with those I love ..."*

Ideally your professional and personal life should support and strengthen one another. Consider ways to find a balance, that will increase the quality of your life whether for family, study, interests, fun, socialising, or relaxation. Having time and energy to focus on the activities you enjoy, and your relationships is crucial for your wellbeing. Creating a separation between work and home life is likely to reduce the stress of one area impacting the other. Even small changes to your work arrangements can make a big difference.

Consider these suggestions:

Adopt the "deal with it once" idea!

If thoughts about your never-ending "to do list" keep flooding your brain non-stop, try just looking at it once:

- Decide what to do with something whilst it is in front of you.
- Don't lose your time evaluating and re-evaluating your "to do" list, papers, emails, and tasks and tell yourself that you'll get to it later.
- Decide whether to finish it, delegate it or put it on a special project list.
- Tackle your piles of papers and your emails and tasks in the same way: either use it, file it or delete it.

Are you spending too much time watching TV?

Has watching TV become the default activity when you get home at the end of the day? It's understandable - it's easy. The problem here is that it is also passive, which means that you are not feeding your brain – you are vegetating!

I am not suggesting that there is nothing worth watching. There are indeed some programs that provide entertainment, information and food for thought that have excellent value. However, there is also a lot of pulp that just fills hours.

There is a place for chilling out in front of the TV when you're tired and don't have much energy left to give, but generally it is wise to cut down on the amount of TV you watch as it will insidiously sap your time.

There are some staggering statistics revealed by polls on the amount of TV watching. According to data released by Nielsen in 2016[27], American adults watch an average of 5 hours and 4 minutes of television per day. That's a lot of wasted hours... I wonder if Australia is far behind? I wonder what the 2020 statistics are showing?

The habit of watching TV starts at a young age and unfortunately, in some families, the television has become the unofficial nanny, keeping children glued to it while parents do things they need to do. This also poses an important question is: Whose values are the children absorbing? Consider also that some TV content gives questionable morals to our children. These are hours that you (and your children) could have spent doing something positive, empowering, creative or useful. It's preferable that *you* influence your children rather than the TV they watch!

Another point to make is that late at night the blue light that emanates from the screen will affect your ability to get off to sleep. There is also the hype and noise from some TV shows which can be disturbing, if not draining.

So be selective and discriminating about what you choose to watch, as much of the content does not feed your brain.

Does it really entertain?
Does it really inform?

Many people think that watching The News is depressing – I am one of them. It is not that I prefer to be ignorant of what is going on in the world. I am simply discriminating about the sources I receive information from.

---

27 https://www.nytimes.com/2016/07/01/business/media/nielsen-survey-media-viewing.html

STOP WATCHING SO MUCH TV and find alternatives!

Wean yourself off.

Go cold turkey and just stop!

Focus on healthier habits instead!

Build a healthier self-esteem (remove the influence of unrealistic expectations and comparisons!)

Focus on your social interactions instead of solitary activities

Increase your productivity

Sharpen your thinking processes

Stop being sedentary: live healthier

Cancel your cable subscription and save money too!

Be a better role model for your children.

Finding More Time

Here are 25 practical suggestions: (understand that some ideas are recurring ... the theme of *priority* is a good example.) There is no 'order of importance' in this list of points. Some things will be more meaningful to some people than others.

1. **Be present**: turn off your phone when you are with your loved ones. Focus on them. Eat together. Relax and unwind together. Exercise together.

2. **Let go of perfectionism.** It doesn't exist and you will only wind up frustrated. The healthier option is to strive not for perfection, but for *excellence!*

3. **Prioritise** your work tasks. Determine the most urgent tasks for the day and allocate sufficient time to complete them. It is important that you do not let the stress build so that you are het up when you get home and cannot focus or be present.

4. **Be more efficient** in completing your work: group similar tasks together and you will get into the swing of it. You won't feel like you're swapping and changing all the time.

5. **Say 'no' to certain requests.** Working for longer does not necessarily mean you are being productive – in fact the opposite is true. Sometimes you may want to say 'no' and that's ok.

6. **Take regular breaks.** Don't rely on days off from a demanding job to refresh yourself – take breaks during your workday. You will be more productive and focussed if you reduce your stress. It is a healthy habit to socialise with others during your breaks and go for a walk to stretch and get your circulation going.

7. **Unplug** on your days off. Strive for satisfying downtime (away from work). It is a sure-fire way to feel like you are achieving a healthy balance. Shut off from technology sometimes. Limit the amount of work you do at home - including responding to phone calls, texts, and emails. Successfully switching on and off from work will help you de-stress and sleep better.

8. **Reduce your work hours.** If this is possible and you are able to work four days per week – what might you be able to achieve?

9. **Use technology to work more efficiently.** Can an email exchange replace the need for a meeting? Can video calls for meetings achieve the same? Can working from home occasionally create more time – especially if you have a lengthy commute?

   Be aware that the flipside to using technology to be more efficient is that you can suffer overwhelm when you can't get through all your emails etc. Be aware of this and remember to always **focus on the priority!**

10. **Recreation**: don't waste your annual holidays: use them to unwind, **refresh** your attitude and **recharge** your batteries.

11. **Outsource the repetitive tasks in your life** and learn to let other people help. Depending on your circumstances, getting a housekeeper, a PA or a cook is a great example.

12. **Go for the priority!** Be mindful of time-wasting people and time-wasting activities.

13. **Build on your small successes**. Make a list of priority changes that you need to make and do it "step by step".

14. **Don't try to be all things to all people.** This has been mentioned before but it is such a gem (and repetition is good!!) so putting it to you again: say "No" sometimes. Don't just manage to fill up your schedule with 'stuff' when it may not be serving your goals or state of happiness. Don't feel like you have to give an excuse – just say that you can't do it.

15. **Focus on your strengths** and outsource the other things that you're not expert at.

16. **Ask for help** when you need it.

17. **Remove distractions** if they get in the way of completing tasks: turn off your phone, radio, TV, go to a quiet place.

18. **Reward yourself** for accomplishing your steps and goals.

19. **Step by step approach.** Start with your most important goal and chunk it down into 'doable' steps so that you can get it done - step by step. By working on your most important project first while you have the energy and headspace, you'll feel energised to keep the momentum going. Also, the less important things that you need to do may not require as much concentration or focus.

20. **Multi-tasking** is hugely useful but understand that some tasks combine well, and others don't, so be smart about what you can combine, i.e. talk to a friend on the phone whilst you're on your exercise bike or preparing the dinner, do your manicure whilst listening to music or a podcast.

21. **Diarise** consistently: so that you know when deadlines or events are approaching. It will also remove a lot of mental stress and worry.

22. **Delegate**: Value yourself - only do the high-priority things!

23. **Embrace organisation:** keep your workspace (and your home) free from clutter.

24. **Don't waste time** on being negative.

25. **Keep orientated**: keep your eye firmly on the ball (your goals).

Everyone alive has the same amount of time - 24 hours a day - to spend as they wish.

Everyone alive has the same amount of time - 24 hours per day - to spend as they wish. So, now is the time to figure out what matters the most to you and spend your days, hours and minutes, doing *those* things. Don't waste time - your most precious resource - by not being mindful!

American Pulitzer prize winning author Annie Dillard [28] makes this insightful and thought-provoking statement:

"How we spend our days is of course, how we spend our lives.

What we do with this hour, and that one, is what we are doing."

This is a great reminder that our reality may not be what we want for ourselves, so it is time to reassess and make some changes if you want to experience a different reality!

With that in mind, let's now order *your* priorities. Use a computer for this so that you can edit and rearrange as you decide on the appropriate hierarchy of your life priorities.

Here is your homework:

Life Priority Analysis - Worksheet

1. **Just Start:**
   Start a new page and start writing. Do not worry about ordering things at this point. Just write down all the things that you value and want to get done.
   Some examples:
   Finish my Uni degree (diploma, course, certificate etc.)
   Renovate my house (apartment, garden, bathroom, investment property...)
   Lose 15kg of weight
   Quit smoking
   Reduce my alcohol consumption to (1/day, only on weekends?...)
   Learn the Italian language
   Buy a house (car, holiday, ...???)
   Have a child.

---

[28] Learn more about this inspiring writer: http://www.anniedillard.com/

DONNA PORTLAND

Teach my kids to play soccer (cricket, rugby, tennis, bowling)
Take up a new and fulfilling hobby or sport.
Write as many as you can think of!

2. **Start to order the importance of your life priorities**. If it is hard for you to decide then just compare two and decide which is more important. As yourself *"If I could attain only one of these two aims, which would it be?"* That is your highest priority. Move it up or down according to your decision. Then go to the next one and compare to the one you have currently ranked as highest and do the same. Repeat the process until you're finished. You will find that some things will stay at the top of the list and others drop down. When you have your list in order you can proceed.

3. Ask yourself *"What has gotten in the way?"* (for each example). What has prevented you from seeing this through? Think of all the reasons you have given yourself for why you haven't started or haven't given it the time it needs, or have just given up...?

Examples:

Finish my Uni degree	I got bogged down at work – making a living. I have to take the kids to sport each weekend. My parents are sick and need my attention. My wife works fulltime so I have to do an equal share of the domestic chores.
Renovate my house	I have so many other things going on in my life that I can't see how I could set aside enough time to start the project and get it finished. I feel tired most of the time so I can't be bothered to start something and keep the momentum going.
Quit smoking	When I get stressed I rely on cigarettes to calm me down....
Lose 15kg of weight	I have so much going on that I am too tired to devote time to exercise. So, I find myself sitting on the couch watching TV instead because I don't have the energy or drive to go to the gym. I have been so distracted with things going on in my life that I still haven't made an appointment with a nutritionist/ dietitian to work out the best diet plan to achieve my goal.
Add yours...	
...	

If you honestly can't see where your time has gone it might help you to do this: Track what you do during the week:

Examples: Hours spent each day

Activity	M	T	W	T	F	S	S	Total
Working at my job								
Reading Books								
Hanging with friends								
Watching TV								
Shopping/Cooking/Eating								
Domestic chores (cleaning, laundry, garden, etc.)								
Play with Social Media / internet surfing								
Exercising								
My hobbies								
Chatting on the phone								
Family time								
Relaxation time								
Partner / relationship time								
Smoking								
At the pub with mates								
Add to this list so that you can see where you are spending your time...								

Work out your totals and find out where you are putting in your time (or wasting it on something that isn't contributing to the successful completion of your goals). In this way you can find out where the imbalances lie.

4. Ask yourself: *"How much time do I need to achieve my priorities?"* (per day / per week / per month)?

DONNA PORTLAND

Examples:

Finish my Uni degree	If I do it part-time I need 4hrs/week for lectures, 2 hrs/week for tutorials, 4 hrs week for study.....)
Renovate my house	If I structure the renovation in stages I can get one thing done and then go onto the next. I would need 30 hours a month to achieve a 'room by room' approach.
Lose 15kg of weight	I need 45-60 mins per day to either walk or go to the gym. It takes the same amount of time to eat healthy food choices as it does to eat unhealthily ...
Quit smoking	Smoking just saps my time. I get distracted from what I was doing to go outside for a cigarette, and it takes me a while to focus back on my task. Consider also that I spend 5-7 minutes on each cigarette, a pack of 25 will take way more than 2-hrs of my time. So, if I quit I will gain all that time back!

Can you see where you might be able to shift from the time you've spent doing a low priority action and put that time towards a high priority action?

5. Ask yourself: *"What Resources (and options) do I have to assist me in finding time for my priorities?"*

Examples:

Finish my Uni degree	Start with just one subject per semester – plus summer school. Before long you will become used to the 10-hrs per week commitment and barely notice. It may even seem not that much of a stretch to add another subject next semester! Get through your reading list when you are on holiday – lying on your sunbed!
Renovate my house	Delegate some aspects of the job to skilled tradesmen (or AirTasker or HiPages et al). Get good advice before you start the job so that you don't waste time fixing mistakes! Consult people you know who have done the same thing and ask them for their tips.

Lose 15kg of weight	Use a meal delivery service to (a) save loads of time shopping, preparing, cooking, and cleaning up after a meal. (b) achieve a controlled calorie meal at the same time!
	Take the dog for a walk more often and for longer periods - get more steps into your day! Be efficient – do two things at the same time: chat on the phone with a friend (or your mum) while you walk the dog (*and* get exercise!)
	Ride your bike to do small shops – instead of driving and increase your exercise minutes whilst you fulfil your shopping mission.
	The more weight you lose the more likely you will regain your energy so making this a priority is wise and will have a positive knock-on effect on the momentum of your other goals.
Quit smoking	Depending on what you have previously tried in order to give up, try a fresh approach. Consider Hypnosis – works for me! The two hours you invest getting therapy may be the best two hours that you have ever spent!

6. Ask yourself: "*What can I delegate – so that I have more time (and energy) for my priorities?*"

Some ideas:

Outsource your domestic cleaning rather than doing it yourself.

Same for weeding and mowing – unless you turn the gardening into exercise or do it yourself because you find it relaxing!

Try home delivered meals for a while: see how much time it saves and whether it ticks other (weight loss) boxes.

Organise with other parents at your children's school to take turns (car-pooling) the kids to sport or to school.

The suggestions may seem like a bit of work, but it will be very revealing for you to see where you have been giving your time away and where you can gain it back! I am excited for you that you are soon going to be able to give yourself a big gift. Once you get clear on what you want and can see the big picture of how you can get there, it is easy to then see the steps you need to take to make it happen. Then you do it! Live it and enjoy it.

CHAPTER 12

KNOWLEDGE IS POWER OR IS IT?

Consider the quote by bestselling author Napoleon Hill: **"Knowledge is only potential power. It becomes power only when, and if, it is organized into definite plans of action, and directed to a definite end."**

Hill is saying that it is all very well to know something, but to act on it is the key to the knowledge having power. This makes perfect sense. It's just academic if you don't use the knowledge.

Author, speaker and leadership expert Robin Sharma [29] echoes the idea: **"Knowledge is only potential power. For the power to be manifested, it must be applied."**

Often when I speak to friends or work with clients, we discuss or agree on potential solutions to their issues and very often they remark that they did know what they should be doing, but just didn't follow through ... So clearly they had the knowledge, but the problem was that they chose to not apply that knowledge. Clearly knowledge is not powerful unless we use it.

---

[29] https://www.robinsharma.com/ A *very* interesting person – it is well worth exploring his writings and videos.

"Knowledge is only potential power. It becomes power only when, and if, it is organized into definite plans of action, and directed to a definite end."

Napoleon Hill

"Knowledge is only potential power. For the power to be manifested, it must be applied."

Robin Sharma

TAKE ACTION

It is a wonderful idea to read and learn, listen to experts, experiment, gain expertise and specialised knowledge, **but you need to ACT on that knowledge** to make it real and use its power to produce wonderful results for your life, relationships, and for your business or career.

Donna Portland

Suggestions for how to gain knowledge that you can then choose to use:

set aside time every day to learn more from those who know and pursue what is true for you.

Read, Read, and Read some more.

You can learn so much from others! Benefit from their experience and discoveries, their insights, and learnings. All successful people read as much as possible to feed their brains.

There are so many benefits to reading: mental stimulation, stress reduction, obtaining knowledge, expanding your vocabulary, improving your memory, strengthening your analytical skills, improving your focus and concentration, and generally improving your writing skills, tranquillity, and it's free entertainment!

Reading is something you can do any day, anytime, anywhere, alone or with others - not just when you need to. Set aside 20-30 minutes each day or more if you can manage. Turn your reading habit into the valuable life tool that it can become!

If you are more of an auditory type learner, then try:

Podcasts, YouTube clips...

Any time you are doing something less than mentally stimulating, i.e. driving, riding the train or bus to work, walking the dog, doing your laundry, you can easily wear your headphones and listen to a podcast at the same time. Pick your subject of interest - there are many to choose from and ENJOY!

If you are more of a kinaesthetic type learner, then try:

Experiential learning opportunities...

It is great to educate yourself through first-hand experience. There are four main elements which operate in a continuous cycle during the learning experience: concrete experience, reflective observation, abstract conceptualisation, and active experimentation.

Skills, knowledge, and experience can be acquired outside of the traditional classroom setting, and may include brainstorming sessions, group buzz sessions, debates, simulations and gaming, role-playing, performance and artistic productions, job shadowing, fellowships, field trips and excursions, field research, apprenticeships, internships, bootcamps and hackathons, co-ops, incubators and accelerators, studies abroad, volunteering and service-learning projects.

Remember: Learn and gather knowledge: then use it!

"The smallest of actions is always better than the noblest of intentions."

— Robin Sharma

Important Considerations:

- Never stop learning! but use your expertise and specialised knowledge in a strategic and organised way.

- Don't get sucked into fads or emotional responses. Use your intuition (*not* your emotions) to judge what is useful.

- Not everyone who professes to be an expert is authentic. Use your intuition before accepting their ideas.

- Procrastinate with purpose: think well about important things before acting!

CHAPTER 13

WHO DO YOU SPEND YOUR TIME WITH?

In a previous chapter you evaluated *where* you spend your time and how much of it you waste! Now, it's time to think about the people who you associate with, as they have an enormous influence.

> ***"Show me the five people you spend the most time with and I'll show you who you are".***

This statement has been attributed to the late motivational speaker Jim Rohn [30]. It is quite a dramatic statement, but it does stand to reason. We have all experienced in our lives how the words and behaviours of the people we hang out with rubs off on us over time. You start to like the same things, say the same things, do the same things and even start to believe the same things. A classic example is how teenagers often find themselves doing the wrong kind of things once they start hanging out with a bad crowd.

There has been much discussion on the concept of proximity causing influence and there are compelling research arguments to suggest strong correlations. Intuitively though you can feel the truth of the statement. However, I think that the influence is far wider than "the *five* people you spend the most time with". Research suggests that we are also influenced by people we have never even met, for example marketers and advertisers, authors, journalists, politicians, actors, and musicians. Influence is everywhere! It is in the myriad words and messages that we are receiving every day via multiple channels.

Who (and what) do you read, watch, and listen to?

You have some control over those 'outside' channels as you have full choice in what, and how often you subscribe, to that input. Now I have mentioned that I am no fan of listening

---

[30] https://www.jimrohn.com/ This man was a phenomenal teacher for personal development, communication, and leadership.

to The News. I get this distinct feeling that many journalists are grinding their particular axe or are kowtowing to the persuasion of the entity they are employed by. I know that there are also many journalists who have integrity and try to represent the facts and the truth, but of course it is all subjective. The question I ask is how can we distinguish the facts from the spin?

You *do* have complete control over who you let into your life as a friend, teacher, or mentor. Perhaps, as I did, you can run a filter and honestly evaluate all the people in your life in this context:

Do they often whinge and complain?

Do they sometimes feel toxic?

Do they put you down? kill your dreams? hurt you? abuse you? use you for their own convenience? manipulate you? deceive you? be judgemental about you or others? etc.

Is any of their behaviour narcissistic?

> *[Narcissists are people who have an inflated sense of their own importance, a deep need for excessive attention and admiration, exaggerating their achievements, talents and importance, arrogant thinking and behaviour, troubled relationships, jealousy, and a lack of empathy for others and consideration for other people. They may show an excessive interest in or admiration of self and their physical appearance. Other words to describe may include: vain, in love with self, self-admiring, wrapped up self, self-absorbed, self-obsessed, conceited, self-centred, self-regarding, egotistic, egoistic, egocentric, egomaniac...]*

If you take a long and honest look at the people in your life you will be able to identify who contributes to your well-being and who doesn't. Then it is your choice what to do next. It may not be easy to move away from those people, but you will need to make it happen if you want to step away from their negative influence.

Long periods of living with a narcissist, for example, will cause you to change your behaviours to avoid conflict; so you back down in arguments, you agree - just to keep the peace, you avoid 'touchy' subjects, tread on eggshells, you don't express yourself freely, you become a 'groupie', you drop most your friends because they weren't approved of by the narcissist, you bend over backwards to keep them happy, you get used to playing second fiddle, you get used to being yelled at and put down and you start to view it as normal ... you get the picture - it's not healthy!

DONNA PORTLAND

What next?

I faced this question myself after I had finished taking inventory of my 'friend list'. I decided that I needed to build my friendship list back up, as I had neglected them over the years. I had become isolated. So, I reconnected with a lot of people that I had lost contact with - to see if friendship might be still there. The fact is that we are all on the same path, but just at different stages or levels of understanding about that path! I am more interested in connecting with people who are always moving forward and asking questions about life, than those who have chosen to stay the same.

"If you are not growing, you are dying."

This quote has been attributed to a number of people, Lou Holtz, Marcus Lemonis, Tony Robbins, and Morihei Ueshiba.

In my opinion they all got it right!

I seek out new people, new friends wherever I am. Since I value and appreciate the importance of learning and growing and reaching my mission in life, I have tended to find people on a similar path. I approach people in an open, honest, and unapologetic way. I have also been conscious of the need to keep my energy raised and a smile on my face. People respond well to authenticity. So, if you're feeling happy it shows and people respond.

I have been selective and have only let in the people who reach my standards. Let me clarify that statement because I want to be clear that the goal here is not to look for perfection in people - that doesn't exist. I personally look for humility, presence, empathy, an enquiring and open mind, intelligence, kindness and caring, good social skills and the mindset of having fun and enjoying life. These friends are not 'all about money and success'. There is nothing wrong with money at all, and success is self-defined, so can be quite different amongst individuals.

The distinction I am making is that the accumulation of possessions and money *for its own* sake is empty and unfulfilling. It turns out that there is never enough - no matter how much money you make. Life becomes a big mission to make more money whilst the most meaningful and satisfying aspects of life are largely swept to the side. The way I see it now is that it is better to have less (friends), but higher quality friendships, than many friends who are not positive influences or not progressing their lives and yours.

In terms of teachers and mentors I am inviting in those who can assist me to hone my skills and progress my life in the direction that I want to go - towards joy and fulfilment.

Similarly to how I appointed a personal training coach to help me get fit and lose weight, and how I have chosen life coaches who have assisted me to find my focus and take action, I also have a business coach to guide me through various modern-day marketing methods that I don't have much experience with, and even less interest in, so that I can reach my professional goals.

The smart move is to seek mentors who will assist you with your learning and growth. A good mentor will coach, motivate, challenge, protect you from taking the wrong steps, advise and share.

Sir Isaac Newton said:

> ## *"If I have seen further than others, it is by standing on the shoulders of giants."*

He is saying that none of us can 'do,' 'go' or 'be' all we can be all by ourselves! We need to ask for help. No one is an island. You will require other people's help, support, insight, feedback, and resources at some point in your journey, and perhaps many times over. Mentors provide counsel and resources that are not necessarily accessible or readily available. Mentors can help you to extend your vision and they enable their protégés to attain greater heights. Don't be afraid to approach someone and ask their opinion or ask for their assistance. You have nothing to lose and everything to gain!

CHAPTER 14

MONEY AND YOUR FINANCES

Money and finances are a big concern for many people throughout their lives. They worry that they will have enough money to live a comfortable life and have freedoms, provide for and take care of their family, pay their living expenses, be able to cope if misadventure or disease strikes, and even to survive in some cases.

I certainly needed to educate myself when I became single after so many years of deferring most of the financial responsibilities to my partner. Big mistake! Firstly, it is *your* money, so you need to understand where it is and what it's doing. Secondly, much as you would like to trust people, it is not always a good idea. Two heads (making decisions) are better than one anyway. So always be involved with your financial situation and make informed decisions.

Much has been written on the subject of making money and managing finances, so no need to reinvent the wheel here. It's also not my specific area of expertise, so I just want to highlight four pillars of good general financial advice regarding taking care of your money, that, if you haven't thought about yet, would be wise to do so - the sooner the better. I have compiled this from extensive reading and research and amalgamated the information here.

1. Plan Your Financial Future.
2. Save a portion of what you earn.
3. Pay off your debt.
4. Invest wisely.

1. Plan Your Financial Future.

Although I hold a Diploma of Financial Markets, I am not a financial planner so cannot give specific advice. You need to visit a trained and impartial financial planner if you haven't already. Financial Planning is a specific skill set and specialised knowledge.

Professional financial advisors can help you:

- identify short, medium, and long-term goals
- develop strategies to achieve your financial goals
- manage your money wisely/effectively
- make the most of your superannuation
- work out your insurance needs
- develop an investment plan
- diversify your investments
- choose tax-effective investments
- discover if you are eligible for any government assistance
- plan for your retirement
- consider your estate planning needs.

A licensed financial adviser can help you identify realistic goals and put strategies in place to achieve them.

Everyone has a unique financial situation and therefore has different needs. You should determine your needs before you decide what kind of financial advisor to work with. That way, you can decide if they are a good fit for you before you even meet them. While you are searching, remember that "Financial Advisor" and "Financial Planner" are broad categories. Ideally you want to find someone who has experience working with clients in situations similar to your own. Ask your colleagues, friends and family for referrals and also search online. Check their credentials and reviews before you make an appointment.

Certified Financial Planners (CFP) have a fiduciary duty to work in their clients' best interests. A Financial Planner specialises in creating a comprehensive plan to help you achieve your long-term goals. They must follow a code of ethics and conduct, meaning they must always provide advice based on your best interests instead of their own (the products that provide the biggest commissions!). Go online to find an CFP near you or to verify an advisor's certification.

A Financial Advisor refers to anyone who helps their clients manage their money. Think of it as an umbrella that other terms fall under. Advisors may specialise in investment management, estate planning, retirement planning, insurance, debt repayment, tax planning or any other aspect of the financial industry. They might even help you with each of these things. Advisors may also cater to certain income levels. Ultra-high-net-worth individuals may want to consider working with a Private Wealth Manager, while someone struggling to get out of debt may prefer the help of a Financial Counsellor.

There are times when you can make your own financial decisions.

At other times it is reassuring to be able to consult a professional.

Getting financial advice can help you plan and manage your big financial decisions.

Remember that financial advice costs: Find out about the cost of advice and understand what you are paying for. Make sure the adviser does not receive any sales incentives for recommending particular products.

2. Save a portion of what you earn.

The 10% savings rule says you should save about 10% of your income for retirement. If you have no idea how much to save, it gives you a starting place, but this is NOT a one-size-fits-all-rule; more of a general guideline that may work for you. Everybody has a different financial situation, different ages, marital situations, pension amounts, careers, risk tolerances, expenses, etcetera. There is no way one savings rule can apply to all those different situations.

If you are a high-income earner, you should save much more than 10% of your income if you want to maintain a similar lifestyle in retirement. An alternative to saving more would be a planned lifestyle downsizing once you retire: a smaller home, less expensive cars, more home cooking, and so on.

As a rule of thumb, the more money you make, or the later you start saving, the more you need to save. If you started saving in your early twenties and consistently saved 10% of everything you made, the 10% savings rule would work. But how many twenty-somethings do that?

Many people find themselves in their mid-forties or fifties when they first give serious thought to saving for retirement. If that's you, and your career is doing well, a 10% savings rate is probably not going to be enough. But 10%, or any amount of regular savings, is better than none.

Obviously if you have superannuation, the predicted amount at retirement will differ from person to person and be subject to the state of the share market. You will need to balance this with your other savings and investments.

3. Pay off your debt.

Q: Should you save money or pay off debt?

A: Think of it this way: since credit card interest rates are very often much higher than savings interest rates, you end up spending more money on debt interest than you would earn on your savings investment.

If you have found yourself in a situation where you are struggling to pay off multiple debts it can feel overwhelming. The best place to start is by putting a plan together for repaying your debts. Start with a budget, once you have that built and know how much you can repay, think about strategy.

Here's how to get started:

When it comes to credit cards:

- Pay off as much as you can every month to reduce interest. Make sure you pay at least the minimum monthly repayment to avoid late payment or default fees.

- When choosing which credit card to get rid of first, think about paying off the credit card with the highest interest rate first. In addition to making minimum payments on all cards, pay more on the card with the highest interest rate, so you pay off the total amount on that card first. Then work your way through your other cards.

- Stop using all but one of your credit cards and try to only use it for emergencies.

- Move your debts across to a balance transfer credit card with a lower interest rate for a set period.

- Get debt help if you need it. If you are having problems juggling your debts, it is important to act quickly to get help. If you just ignore it, you may have difficulty obtaining credit in the future if your credit rating is negatively affected.

  There are two ways to go if you need help with your debts:

  - Contact your credit provider straight away. You may be able to organise an agreed repayment plan until you pay off your debt or until a temporary financial problem is resolved.

  - Get help from a financial counsellor. This is usually a free service and they can help you sort out your debts.

Make necessary sacrifices
(and delay gratification!)

4. Invest wisely.

Warren Buffet, the most famous investor of our time, advises:

"Rule number one with money is <u>don't lose it.</u>
 Rule number two: don't forget rule number one."

Get advice. Make considered investments: thoroughly look at the downside as well as the upside of any investment. Understand all aspects of your investment – don't jump in.

How to choose your investments?

First you need to determine your risk profile:

Risk is a fundamental part of finance and investing. Therefore identifying, quantifying, and assessing risk needs to be the first step in the investment process. Risk profiling is a process that advisers use to help determine the optimal levels of investment risk for their clients. The aim is to identify the risk required to meet your investment objectives, your risk capacity, and your tolerance to risk. This relationship is shown in the described below.

Risk Required - refers to the level of risk required to be taken on investments to achieve your desired level of investment return.

Risk Capacity - refers to the level of investment risk (or losses) that you can afford to take.

Risk Tolerance - refers to the level of risk you're comfortable taking.

Through this process, a risk profile is created which will govern future decision making and help determine the appropriate asset allocation strategy for your investment portfolio.

"Rule number one with money is **don't lose it.**

Rule number two: don't forget rule number one."

Warren Buffet

DONNA PORTLAND

Here are 6 indicative risk profiles:

Risk Averse: Defensive 95-100% / Growth 0-5 %
The defensive investor seeks consistent income return with only a small proportion of growth assets. If the risk tolerance is zero then the investment will be a cash account.

Conservative: Defensive 85% / Growth 15%
A conservative profile seeks to conserve wealth rather than aim for capital growth. This generally suits older investors who do not want to risk losing their money, since they have little or no more working capacity.

Moderate: Defensive 70% / Growth 30%

Growth: Defensive 30% / Growth 70%

Aggressive: Defensive 15% / Growth 85%
An aggressive profile may seek financial gain despite the risks associated with the investments, generally suiting younger investors who have plenty of opportunity to earn an income over many years in the workforce.

Very Aggressive: Defensive 0% / Growth 100%

Consider, investing in yourself...!

Don't just invest your money into financial products - consider investing in yourself?

You would no doubt be familiar with the concept of spending money to make money? You can choose to invest wisely in yourself to improve your employment opportunities and career prospects. It is not a guarantee however, an investment in yourself for further education etc. is a calculated risk, and your strategy and plans need to be well considered, that they will achieve your objective. So, get advice and procrastinate with purpose: think well about important things before acting!

CHAPTER 15

YOUR HIGHER SELF - THE SPIRITUAL PATH

As individual beings, we experience the feeling of distinctness and separateness from each other. Throughout life it can feel like we are competing with others: with our siblings for our parents' attention, with our classmates for the best grades, with other people for jobs (money, prestige, lovers, resources, and so on). We notice the vast differences in the fortunes of others compared to ourselves, and it can seem that each living creature's existence is a fight for its own survival, in many cases at the expense of other living creatures. This is the undeniable reality.

I was fairly fortunate however, blessed with intelligence and having received a good education, I also learned a variety of vocational skills and was always able to make a viable living. My ethic was always to work efficiently and diligently.

I received the usual 'prescription' for life: "*...study hard, get good grades, get a good job, find a partner, settle down, buy a house, have a family and live happily ever after!"*

That's what did, but to be honest down the track it wasn't working out so well. I was living inauthentically and unconsciously, and the reality was no blissful 'happily ever after' for this little black duck!

The truth was that for most of my life I had allowed myself to get swept along with whatever was going on. My head was turned one way and then the other. I was always flat chat busy and constantly distracted. I never felt that I had any control of what was happening in my life. I just responded to whatever occurred and did the best I could at the time to make the best of it. My plate was always full to overflowing with things to do, places to go and people to see. It was a whirlwind. To my credit I mostly got it all done! I know that various friends wondered how I managed. Over time however, since I neglected to feed my soul, I fell out of love, and I became somewhat depressed, unconscious, and undirected.

Look around you. I'll bet that you know plenty of people who live the same way. Maybe *you* do - or did! People who live unconsciously just 'clock on' and 'clock off' each day. They get through it but are not really satisfied or present. They are definitely not living joyously - perhaps only for fleeting moments. Mostly time just races by and we remark *"where did the time go...?"* and *"Oh $#!& - not another birthday...!"*

For me that was not a good place to be. **Something was missing. I didn't feel whole. I felt disconnected - separate.**

My life lacked joy and purpose. I tried to fit in and make an effort, but I was just going through the motions. It didn't work. The evidence showed on face, and my body: I put on lots of weight and looked haggard. I found myself in a bad mood often. Hey, very often I was no fun at all!

When I finally got some clarity and realised the direction that my life had taken I decided to make changes; to live with intention and make mindful efforts and endeavours to care for myself and others, as well as the environment. As I have mentioned throughout this book, I have done this by making small daily changes to my habits and have gotten in touch with my higher self to tap into my intuition, kindness, love and resources that I have within. This is within all of us.

I have found my energy and capacity for living a fulfilled life. You can do the same because everything you need is within you now.

A funny thing happened to me recently that illustrates that point and made me smile. My driver's licence was expiring, and I had to go to the motor registry to renew it and this involves taking a photo. The attendant offered that I could keep the previous photo if I wanted to since it had been only five years, but I chose to take a new one. We did that and then completely out of the blue when the photo came up on his screen, he smiled and said to me "It's a *much better* photo this time anyway!" That's more proof that I have changed a lot in five years and rather than looking five years older (and wrinklier) as you would expect, I looked "*much better*". I felt better too!

On my journey, after I had regained my physical health and energy, I then concentrated on addressing my mindset. I needed my energy back first so that I could approach, and maintain, my journey.

Where to start? I gained my answer from the sages.

Jesus Christ said:

"Ask, and it will be given you. Seek, and you will find. Knock, and it will be opened for you. For everyone who asks receives. He who seeks finds. To him who knocks it will be opened."   (Matthew 7:7-8[31])

---

[31] Taken from the World English Bible https://biblehub.com/matthew/7-7.htm

Buddha said:

"When the student is ready, the teacher will appear."

A useful proverb of unknown origin declares:

"Everything you need is within you now."

The trick here is to see it and feel it! The magic - the sense of this statement - will happen if you allow yourself to believe that you are enough - just as you are!

"Ask, and it will be given you.
Seek, and you will find.
Knock, and it will be opened
for you. For everyone who asks
receives. He who seeks finds. To
him who knocks it will be opened."

Jesus Christ (Matthew 7:7-8)

"When the student is ready,
the teacher will appear."

Buddha

"Everything you need
is within you now."

Proverb, Unknown origin.

I wanted to *feel* that I was enough. My overarching goal was to find my joy for life again. I wanted to become the best version of myself and rediscover my laughter and joy. I wanted to radiate my positivity. I wanted to be my own best friend and not my worst enemy (and biggest critic).

By the time I got to exploring my spirituality I was already treating myself well. By eating consciously and exercising daily I had lost a lot of weight and regained my fitness and energy. I was healing in many different ways. I was well on the way to reaching my goals, by simply taking one step after another.

Now my search had led me to explore the spiritual side of myself - a part which I had largely ignored until now. I never seemed to have any time for myself. I guess I had just denied the necessity to 'go within' because I had been so distracted and busy all the time. Somehow society discounts the necessity of feeding your soul, as the modern-day fixation on material wealth (as an indication of success) seems to be hugely pervasive. Like many of us, I was influenced to ignore spirituality.

The interesting thing now that meditation is part of my daily life, I no longer feel that I have too much to do, as I had felt previously - all the time … I am more relaxed and see things more clearly. I breathe … and think before I act (or react).

DONNA PORTLAND

What is Spirituality?

Spirituality is a word that is used a lot, but I suspect is often misunderstood. Many people think that spirituality and religion are the same thing, and so they bring their beliefs and prejudices about religion to discussions about spirituality. Though all religions emphasise spiritualism as being part of faith, you can be 'spiritual' without being religious or a member of an organised religion.

There are some pretty clear ways in which religion and spirituality differ.

Religion:

This is a specific set of organised beliefs and practices, usually shared by a community or group. Incorporated are rules and traditions, therefore no scope for different perspectives within an organised religion and those who stray are usually excommunicated, so branch off on their own to start a new version of their religion, yet with the same confines!

It is still possible to explore your spirituality if you subscribe to a particular religion. Think of it as more of a deepening of what is already there.

Spirituality:

Spirituality is not religion.

A more accurate way to think of it is as an alignment of your mental, physical, emotional and spiritual parts coming together.

Spirituality is coming to know who you really are. It is more of an individual practice and is about having a sense of peace and purpose. It also relates to the individual person being able to develop beliefs around the meaning of life and connection with others, without any externally defined values influencing them.

Spirituality is a broad concept with space for many perspectives. Generally, it includes a sense of connection to something bigger than one's self, and it usually involves a search for meaning in life. You could say that it is a universal human experience - something that we all share. People may describe a spiritual experience as a deep sense of aliveness and interconnectedness. Some even use the words 'sacred' or 'transcendent' to describe their spiritual experience.

In terms of connecting with something larger than yourself, some people refer to this as 'God' or 'Spirit' or 'The Source' or 'All That Is' or 'Nature' or 'The Universe', and that it is outside of you. Others feel spirituality is inside of us. In my opinion, it is both.

When it is possible to look beyond the surface of things and see a situation from a different perspective, it is possible to rely on our inner knowing and guidance, and trust that wisdom. This is particularly useful when our lives become challenged and stressed and becoming anxious achieves nothing - in fact, it makes things worse! Anxiety is simply fear of the future - fear of something that hasn't happened yet! It makes no sense.

During difficult times we can find comfort in having a spiritual connection. Our lives become more meaningful and we feel more peace when we know that each of us can support ourselves during times of difficulty. Being able to rely on yourself is very empowering. This has been huge for me: knowing that I don't need anyone else but myself has given me peace. I still want personal connection with others, but it is more of a want than a need. On a deep level I feel connected to all that is/ collective consciousness/ everything/ God/ nature/ the divine/ the universe/ the source ...

Perhaps the reason why people get stressed is that they are looking for an explanation for why things are happening to them? Having a spiritual outlook helps considerably during trying times, as it helps increase our patience to endure whatever is causing the dis-ease and perhaps replace stress with a sense of gratitude. This is why more and more people are exploring their spirituality as they are finding that it is a great way to find (and feel) comfort and inner peace in their lives.

Why should you explore your Spirituality?

Your 'why' is *your* 'why'! Exploring your spirituality means discovering what brings more meaning, purpose or value to your life and makes you feel more connected.

Here are some excellent reasons for 'why':

- Discovering what gives your life meaning
- Getting in touch with what you love
- Finding out what lights up your soul
- Discovering what you are passionate about
- Letting go ... (when you explore you will find plenty of things that will team up with these two words!)
- Going deep and finding tranquillity (despite the madness that life can throw at you)
- Feeling the freedom to get lost in something unexplored
- Improving your relationships/connections with others
- Finding your purpose, i.e. the job that is most satisfying for you, the thing that you are meant to do!

If the 'whys' above appeal to you, then you need to start looking within. It is the only way to get there!

DONNA PORTLAND

Q: How do you embark on your spiritual journey?

A: You start looking!

It is a self-discovery experience. Start reading and researching and see what you find. It *will* be what you need each step of the way.

Perhaps you need a guide or teacher at the start, or along the way of your journey. Bear in mind Buddha's advice regarding spiritual teachers, known as "The Four Reliances":

Rely on the message of the teacher,
not on their personality;

Rely on the meaning,
not just on the words;

Rely on the real meaning,
not just the provisional one;

Rely on your wisdom mind,
not on your ordinary, judgmental mind.

With that sage advice in mind, consider:

Five steps to take to connect to your higher self and spiritual path

1. **Listen to a variety of teachers and let your intuition guide you as to the most useful one for you at that moment of your journey.**

There are many teachers, guides and thought leaders in this space now. More and more people are seeking some form of transformation and growth. They are hungry for answers to life's existential questions. A well-rounded search would include the likes of (in alphabetical order): Allan Watts, Anthony Robbins, Barbara Marx Hubbard, Bob Procter, Brené Brown, Buddha, Deepak Chopra, Eckhart Tolle, Esther Hicks (Abraham Hicks), the Dalai Lama, Jack Canfield, Jaggi Vadudev (Sadhguru), Jesus Christ, John Demartini, John Gray, Louise Hay, Neale Donald Walsch, Neville Goddard, Paul Coelho, Ram Dass, Robin Sharma, Rhonda Byrne, Rumi, Wayne Dyer, and Zig Ziglar. This list is not an exhaustive list by any means but reveals lots of people and places to start listening and reading.

> *"It is by logic that we prove, but by intuition that we discover."*

Henri Poincaré (1854-1912) a French mathematician, theoretical physicist, engineer, and philosopher of science.

2. **Try a variety of techniques to mediate and connect to your higher self.**

Meditation has been well-covered in Part 1 so please refer back if you need to.

There are some excellent guided meditations that you can try to help you connect to your higher self. It is not easy at first, granted. It's the same as anything new that you learn - it takes practice to gain skill and fluency. I can almost hear you asking, *"But which is the best - the quickest and more effective?"* and the answer is the same. You need to start and try different things until you find something that works well for you.

Hypnosis can be extraordinarily useful to reach the subconscious mind to change a lot of bad programming. Some do yoga, or any of two dozen types of meditation. The most important thing to remember is that it needs to be done daily. Aim for at least 20 mins a day or 10-15 mins twice a day. You may have to juggle this with the other things that are happening in your life.

3. **Open your mind to receive your answers.**

Don't listen to people who scoff at your curiosity about meaningful answers to life. It's your journey not theirs! If you allow others to bring you back down, that is where you will stay - as closed-minded as that person. It's not always that they mean to bring you down, it's just that they cannot open their minds and are used to operating a certain way and fear change. Again, that's them and you are you - so just keep on searching and you will find your answers.

Be aware that you can stop listening to the ego - the little voice in your head that keeps rubbishing your enquiring mind. Don't let it sabotage your personal growth!

Remember the saying: "Live and Let Live"

All people should be able to live their lives in the manner they want to, regardless of what others may think.

LIVE

&

LET LIVE

4. **Use your imagination and creativity.**

Imagination and creativity are closely related to intuition but bear further comment. The celebrated photographer Peter Lindberg [32] says:

"Creativity is the basis of self-expression."

Lindberg is right. We create something from with inside ourselves. It starts out as an energy - a thought. It is non-physical. This energy is spiritual and comes from the infinite source (the universe, God, the divine, all that is, the source ...) You can use your imagination - your ability to perceive, sense and create mental images - to create things; tangible and in tangible. Your imagination is infinite and has enormous potential. Your perceptions can become reality if you take action.

5. **Use and trust your intuition to help receive your answers.**

Steve Jobs, founder of Apple, said:

"Don't let the noise of others' opinions drown out your own inner voice. And most important, have the courage to follow your heart and intuition. They somehow already know what you truly want to become. Everything else is secondary."

It is interesting and quite remarkable, that Steve Jobs, the founder of a company built on left brain talent in engineering and analysis, would tout the virtues of intuition! It is a powerful statement to make: *"Everything else is secondary!"*

---

[32] http://www.peterlindbergh.com/

"Don't let the noise of others' opinions drown out your own inner voice.

And most important, have the courage to follow your heart and intuition.

They somehow already know what you truly want to become.

Everything else is secondary."

Steve Jobs, founder of Apple

Before going any further, it should be stated clearly here that intuition does *not* come from a fearful state or a nervous energy. Nor does it come from the conditioning of your mind. Eckhart Tolle says that "**Intuition comes from being present.**" It is not tainted by a negative state like fear or anger. There is a quiet strength behind an intuitive feeling - a peaceful quality in the knowing.

Consider what tuning into your intuition can potentially do for you:

- Feel authentic
- Gain clarity on your life purpose
- Boost your creativity and imagination
- Support your decision-making by augmenting your analytical brain
- Assist you to identify and handle problems more effectively (to reduce stress)
- Keep you safer as you will be more aware of potential threats or danger
- Be open to new ideas that lead to success
- Become sensitive to the energy of the people around you and the environment you are in
- Tune in to others' feelings and thereby improve your relationships
- Boost your confidence in your decisions.

There are many ways to grow and enhance your intuition and here are some that you can start doing and see what works for you. Remember, that any 'muscle' needs strengthening so you need to 'work out' often to develop it.

1. **Meditate**: as mentioned. Do as much as you can manage. If meditation is not possible you can find a quiet space to think, for example, in the shower, at the park, on the train or bus ...

2. **Notice your body's reaction to things**: your 'gut reaction', pain, irregular heartbeat, disease, sweating, and other physical reactions.

3. **Exercise**: this raises your energy and gets you away from the daily grind! Sometimes when you tune out of the left-brain headspace those intuitive thoughts just pop into your head!

4. **Journal**: just empty your brain of the thoughts racing around and spill them all onto paper. They may or may not be useful, but it is highly worthwhile to clear space and get rid of the noise in your head, so that there is room for your intuition to emerge.

   Some people ask themselves specific questions.

   Carry a little notepad with you always so that you can note down any random (and amazing) thoughts that pop into your head.

DONNA PORTLAND

5. **Notice your dreams** which is your subconscious mind processing your thoughts (stresses, judgements, desires, feelings, views, emotions, anxieties, insights, yearnings, and so on). What are your dreams revealing? What is your intuition telling you via your dreams?

6. **Be creative.** You will find a flow when you get into the creative zone and ideas come easily. It is necessary to slow down from being busy long enough to explore this outlet. There are many ways to express your creativity apart from the obvious artistic endeavours. Try playing music, singing, dancing, writing, photography, styling, landscaping, designing, crafts, interior decoration, cooking, mixology, dressmaking, etcetera.

7. **Notice** blasts from the past: whenever thoughts pop into your head notice what comes up. What did you learn? and what insight did you receive from what has happened in your life? Get 20/20 hindsight!

8. Notice sudden feelings that crop up. Don't ignore them. Ask yourself what is the message?

9. Take a sabbatical or a break ...

10. Ask yourself questions and listen for answers. They often come when you are doing something repetitive like the ironing or driving. This happens to me a lot!

11. Assume that your intuitions/feelings are valid: don't fight them even if they are not what you wanted to feel. Listen, don't ignore.

12. Talk with your mentor. This could be an actual person or someone that you talk to in your imagination, like spirit guides.

13. Take a chance - ask a question: flip a coin - see how you *feel* about the answer!

14. Anticipate positive outcomes (instead of negative ones) and see what you can visualise and how that feels. This is not about being 'wishful'.

CHAPTER 16

YOUR PURPOSE

Is there a grand plan to our lives? a destiny? or is our existence empty and meaningless?

This may or may not be a concern for you. Not everyone is concerned with, or believes in, having a 'grand purpose' as such. Most are quite happy to go with the prescribed, traditional model ["...*get a good job, work hard, buy a house, find a partner, and get married, have a family and live happily ever after ...*"] Nothing wrong with that. This seems to work for a lot of people.

One insightful study program that I attended, along my personal development learning path, suggested that life was in fact empty and meaningless ... *unless* you choose to give your life meaning! I am satisfied with that. I can see evidence all over the place of how empty and meaningless many people's lives have become for them. I can also see where people have given their lives purpose. It is definitely a choice that we each have the opportunity to make for ourselves.

It is no surprise that people take very different approaches to living their lives. Some are very contented just living each day - sometimes happy, sometimes not, just getting through it. Some appear to extract from it the most enjoyment they can, whilst others seem to live between one struggle to the next. There is a lot of complaining going on, not a huge amount of satisfaction overall and little sense of freedom. Of course, people's approaches cover a range of attitudes and behaviours. Most of us want to live more happily, with less stress and conflict, more enjoyment, but we find that our reality is not what we would like it to be.

It would be fair to say that I had an 'existential crisis' which caused me to re-think what I was living for and how I was living each day. In existentialist philosophy, the term specifically relates to the crisis of the individual when they realise that their lives are defined by the choices they make. It may cause them to ask "*Why are I living here on Earth? What's it all for? Is this all there is?*" and so on ...

In my case it was provoked by a significant event in my life - the death of a friend. It was not the first time in my life that a close friend had died but this time it made me take stock. He was killed by accident shortly after his 50th birthday and I discovered afterwards that he was not living his life the want he wanted to live it - that he felt stuck. Whilst I grieved it occurred to me how short life can be, how precious it is, how quickly it goes by, and that if you're not living authentically and joyfully then you are wasting your precious time ... wasting your life!

I believe that 'the universe' - the forces that guide our lives - had more in store for me than the life I was living. For a person with a near genius IQ level, I was not making the most of my gifts. Perhaps because I had a low EQ[33].

At that time, I felt that I was wasting my life feeling small and closed in. I would experience episodes of fun and laughter but would then sink back down into the daily grind and the nothingness. I knew on some deep level that I needed to move away from my inertia and put myself 'out there' to find what it is that I was meant to do in this lifetime on Earth. I knew that I had a lot to give but was hiding my light. I did not understand why.

When, and if, you come to this realisation, the big questions become:

"How do I figure out what I am meant to do or become?"

"How will I know when I discover the answer?"

"What happens then...?

A: The answers to the above are different for everyone. These are not simple questions to answer. We each have a unique life journey. Some live blissfully ignorant(?) - oblivious of any need for questions. Others are always asking questions and striving for something. Some reach goals and others don't. There is no 'one way' or 'right way' to live. The answer is that we each need to commit to our own journey for answers and follow our intuition.

The quote from Buddha, which I have mentioned before, is so very relevant here again: ***"When the student is ready, the teacher appears."*** This means that when you commit to opening your mind to receiving the answers you seek; those answers will come. You just need to trust the process. The best advice I can give is that you shouldn't try to hurry

---

[33] IQ is a standardised test of human intelligence. It is a completely different thing to EQ, which measures the capability of an individual to recognise their own emotions and those of others, discern between different feelings, use emotional information to guide thinking and behaviour, and manage or adjust emotions to adapt to environments or achieve their goals.

an answer - just be open to receive it when the time is right – akin to the wisdom of The Supremes' song lyrics "You can't hurry love. You just have to wait!"

I hope you can accept this honest answer. It may be frustratingly vague, but it is also simply true. If you are genuinely searching you *will* find your answers. You will intuitively know when you hit on your answer. You will *feel* the 'rightness' of it. You will also then come to know the next steps that you need to take. You will need to have some faith and take that leap, away from how you have been living life until now.

Connecting to your higher self

Your higher self is the real you, a soul consciousness that is more than just your physicality. Your higher self knows your intentions, desires, and your secrets. Your higher self is the 'you' that is unlimited and eternal. It is the part of you that guides with intuition, excites with inspiration and teaches you through insight.

The mission is to learn how to access your higher consciousness and do it often, as this is your best guide for a meaningful experience of life. The problem is that our busy modern lives seem to demand we spend a lot of our time in survival mode (lower consciousness) paying attention primarily to our external circumstances.

Your higher, spiritual self is always trying to communicate with you.

Have you ever been aware of a powerful feeling or hunch that is trying to guide or steer you towards a particular course of action?

Do you trust your intuition, your perceptions, your 'gut feelings'?

Unfortunately, many people dismiss this because it can't be scientifically measured, but it is definitely valid and meaningful because you can *feel* it, and this personal energy and knowing should not be ignored. These are messages from your higher self which are always trying to restore the light, love, and power to you.

It can be mysterious though, since messages can come via dreams and in unusual ways: the comment of a stranger, a headline caught swiftly before a stranger turns the page of their newspaper, hearing a snippet from a broadcast, a chance meeting with someone you may or may not know, an advert that scoots across your phone or laptop, an overheard conversation where you catch a particularly relevant part that grabs your attention, a voice in your head that makes a suggestion. Sometimes the messages seem weird but sometimes they are clear as day.

The trick is to get used to trusting the voice of your truthful higher self as opposed to the fear-based voice of the ego. Your body can help you decide where the message is coming

DONNA PORTLAND

from. **Since the ego creates its identity around pain and negativity and you feel physical sensations of tension, anxiety, fear, or anger, then you know that the ego is talking.**

You will know if you are talking to the higher self if you feel light, free, happy, love, joy – in other words, you will feel positive energy and wisdom. **The higher self is wise and is always showing you an easier, better, more joyful way to live.**

Your higher self can reveal the illusions, desires and attachments that keep you trapped in a lower vibration. Your higher self will help you to gain a greater ability to recognise limiting, disharmonious, and restricting energies.

The best ways to connect to your higher self is via meditating, journaling, and asking yourself "yes-no" questions and stand by to receive immediate answers. They may even come before you have finished asking! An immediate answer is most likely your higher self as it bypasses the ego and the programming of the mind. Too much analysis gives the ego time to contribute the usual negativity.

When you journal, you are also asking questions and receiving immediate intuitive reactions. Use your physical response as a guide as to what your higher self is revealing.

There are some excellent meditations available to choose from and most are completely free on YouTube, that can assist you to connect with your higher self. The more you get used to doing this, the easier it becomes. Remember that plenty of practice always improves any endeavour.

It is in moments of silence that your higher self can impart to you as much of its wisdom, power, and love that you can receive. When you call upon your higher self, in these moments of silence, take note of the new thoughts you have. Doing this brings you more power, love, wisdom, guidance, abundance, and spiritual vision.

What are your values? and why does it matter?

Tune in to your inner voice (higher self) that tells you whether you are living according to your values. Know what's true for you. If you are not living life the way you want to then it is time to realign your activities with your core beliefs and values. Your goals should match your values for fulfilment.

Where are you already successful? Look and make a list. Consider that self-depreciation is an uninspired life, so reward yourself for your efforts - big and small.

Powerful ideas concerning your life purpose:

Go to your quiet place and think about your life purpose and your mission.

Be aware of "injected values" from society.

Don't conform to what everyone else does without thinking.

Have the courage to live outside the box! Think for yourself.

Don't compare to others as this minimises you.

Be original, in congruency, be inspired and be consistent.

Find unique solutions. Innovate.

Be honest with yourself. Know yourself. Be yourself.

Feed your mind great ideas.

Be grateful for everything in your life.

Orchestrate your life!

Set a strategy and stay with it.

Dedicate - always improve. Never stop learning and growing! This builds personal confidence.

Learn from failure. Whatever happens always ask: How can I learn from this?

CHAPTER 17

YOUR LIFE: TIME TO DECIDE

Do you leave things the same or take action to redirect your life?

There is a reason why you picked up this book and started reading it.

There is a reason that you got all the way through to this chapter. Clearly there are questions that you need to ask yourself: and answer honestly. Let's take stock and then you will have a baseline - a starting point if you like.

WHERE ARE YOU IN YOUR LIFE – RIGHT NOW?

WHAT DO YOU WANT – THAT YOU DON'T CURRENTLY HAVE?

Let's get to work:

Note that it may be best to do this exercise on a computer as you will most likely need to edit your work and arrange things into a specific order once you've reviewed it.

This is for you, and you alone, to discover where you are currently and where you want to be, so put yourself 100% into it. You will get a lot out of this exercise!

Ask yourself:

1. What is my dominant emotion every day?
   How intense are those feelings?

2. What are my primary stressors?

3. Five things that I am tolerating in my life at present:
   (examples: job dissatisfaction, relationship/family stress, financial stress, low self-esteem, personal limitations, etc.)
   And, note how long this has been the situation?

4. What do I *really* want to change in my life?
   Where do I want to go? What is missing?

5. I want to let go of these problem(s) because ...

6. What has driven my life decisions so far?

7. Now get specific: Where am I now?
   What is the reality of my life?
   (Describe how you feel about all aspects of your life and give yourself a rating on a scale of 1-10; 1 being, that you have not made any progress in this area and 10 that you are where you think you should be, at this stage in your life. You can elaborate if you like. It all helps you to get clear on your current state.)

   Adventure: ☐
   Career: ☐
   Emotions: ☐
   Family: ☐
   Finances: ☐
   Health & Vitality: ☐
   Learning & Education: ☐
   Love & Intimacy: ☐
   Personal Growth: ☐
   Relationships - business: ☐
   Relationships - personal: ☐
   Spirituality: ☐
   Time Management: ☐

8. Regarding your answers to the above, pick <u>three</u> areas that you would like to address NOW and makes changes. (You can do this process with all areas if you like, but it is best to approach this in smaller chunks rather than try to deal with everything at once!)

Let's explore what is important to you about those three areas:

Here is an *example*: **Health & Vitality**

<u>Questions:</u>

Can you remember when you were totally motived in that context (area)? Can you remember a specific time?

As you remember that time, recall how you *felt* when you were totally motivated?

Can you name that *feeling*?

What is important to you about that? Write down all the things that you can think of.

Keep going and extract all the feelings associated with that area until you can't think of any more feelings. Push yourself until you start repeating.

Now read those values back to yourself and organise them into the order of importance.

Random values list	*Ordered* values list
Strength	High energy levels
High energy levels	Motivation
Motivation	Self-approval
Sense of achievement	Sense of achievement
Self-approval	Resolve / Discipline
Optimism	Optimism
Sense of personal pride	Strength
Resolve / Discipline	Sense of personal pride

Your turn:

1) _____ (write the **first** area that you would like to address here).

Questions:

Now ask yourself if you can remember when you were totally motived in that context (area)? Can you remember a specific time?

As you remember that time, recall how you felt when you were totally motivated?

Can you name that feeling?

What's important to you about that? Write down all the things that you can think of.

Keep going and extract all the feelings associated with that area until you can't think of any more feelings. Push yourself until you start repeating.

Now read those values back to yourself and organise them into the order of importance.

2) _____ (write the **second** area that you would like to address here).
Apply the questions listed above.

3) _____ (write the **third** area that you would like to address here).
Apply the questions listed above.

Let's keep going:

9. What are my intentions (goals) for the rest of my life?

10. What does 'quality of life' mean to me?
How does it look?
How does it feel?
What does it sound like?

11. Define my **utopia**: (give yourself the freedom to dream big! Treat this like a 'brainstorming' session and let the ideas flow.)

12. The moments when I feel the most complete, satisfied, fulfilled and/or happy are ...
Here are some examples:
  a) *when I help others*
  b) *when I learn something new*

DONNA PORTLAND

     c)   when I develop a skill or ability

     d)   when I reach a goal I've been striving for

     e)   when I face a challenge...

     f)   when I enjoy a moment

     g)   when I'm "in the zone"....

     h)   when ...

13. What is the **payoff** for achieving these goals?
    How is my new life going to be different?
    What is the upside or the reward for following through on these goals?

14. To ensure that I reach my goals I am currently doing:
    (List the actions that you are taking and how often. Note next to each how successful they have been.)

15. The beliefs, fears and/or patterns of behaviours that have prevented me from already achieving my goals are:
    (If you're not sure, then think about if you <u>did</u> know... trust your unconscious mind and write down whatever comes up.)

16. What is the **cost** or the negative consequences for **not** following through?
    What is my life going to be like if I continue to procrastinate, and continue to buy into my excuses, patterns, and fears?

17. **How do I change things?** and break from what is holding me back?

Ah ha... this is the crux. Firstly, you will need to identify your core beliefs and align those with your intentions.

Core Beliefs & Values

Our core beliefs are basic beliefs about ourselves, other people, and the world in general, which we accept as absolute truth without question. Everybody has these deep-seated beliefs which dictate the rules we live by. They determine how we perceive and interpret the world and are very convincing and persuasive and full of conviction. They frame the rules we live by every day. Whenever anything happens, your mind will access the core belief that is most likely to keep you safe and defend you against the world.

Core beliefs are formed in the early years of our lives, and they are based on our experiences and the meaning we gave to those experiences. They comprise our thoughts about the things we see other people do and say, and the advice we are given whilst growing up. They have a direct impact on the way we perceive the world and interpret what happens. It is because these beliefs were formed early in life, that they are child-like and juvenile. There is nothing wrong with youthful thinking, but this thinking lacks understanding and the insight that comes with greater life experience.

Your core beliefs are very important because they determine to what degree your see yourself as acceptable, safe, lovable, competent, powerful, worthy, etc. Of course, crucial to your self-acceptance and self-esteem are your negative core beliefs which have a huge influence on your sense of belonging and the basic picture of how others view and treat you.

Core beliefs affect our judgments of others and as well as our own self-acceptance. So, it is easy to understand the reasons why negative core beliefs can have a huge effect on our sense of self-worth and self-esteem. A common negative core belief is: *"I am not good enough. I'm nothing special. People would not like me if they knew the real me. I don't have enough friends. I'm always having to go to social events on my own. I hate going to parties alone. It's so hard to meet people when you don't know anyone. I always feel uncomfortable, shy, and nervous when I have to introduce myself. No one notices me. I'm terrible at small talk – I never know what to say. So... I don't think I'll go."*

Core beliefs become negative when then get distorted by trauma, and this usually happens during our youth. It is easy to see how people come to see themselves as flawed or unworthy in response to hurt or rejection. Likewise, **if parents neglect to tell their children that they are worthwhile or valued, you can understand how people fail to see value and worthiness in themselves.**

When we believe that we are not good enough - and constantly tell ourselves this - we ignore the positives and focus instead on 'evidence' that it is indeed true. The filters that we apply colour our judgements and the meanings that we give to feelings and words. Since we are predisposed to think this way, that's what we see and hear! Understandably we feel worse and worse, and completely demotivated to change things.

Clearly, it would be equally possible give ourselves opportunities to *disprove* the negative core beliefs and simply remember all the times that we have done well, worked hard, succeeded, connected with others! In that way we can convince ourselves that we *are* good enough. The more positive beliefs will be confirmed, and we are more likely to feel motivated and positively energised.

Positive core beliefs affirm that you *can* make it and *are* good enough! An example of this is *"I am likeable and friendly and have a great smile. I can mix well in any company, and converse well with new people, and my friends and family think that I am good company. I will go and talk to that cute guy (or girl) because I know that I am a good person and worthwhile to know."* If you are saying that to yourself, clearly you don't need to change anything about your positive beliefs!

DONNA PORTLAND

You can see how your core beliefs are the basis of your self-worth.

- They are your rules and dictate what you can and cannot do.
- They are part of your self-talk and contribute to how you interpret the world.

Here are some examples of negative core beliefs that you can change if you decide that they are not correct, that somehow the child you were distorted the feedback or believed erroneously that someone else's opinion was more valid than your own! (think teacher, parent, bully, or anyone...)

Core Belief	Associated Thoughts
☹ I am dumb (bad, stupid, etc.)	I can't do anything right. Things that I do are likely to fail.
☺ I am clever (smart, crafty, shrewd, etc.)	I will succeed and achieve my goals.
☹ I am unlikeable (unattractive, unlovable, ugly, etc.)	Nobody will ever like me. I will always be alone.
☺ I am attractive (amicable, captivating, lovable, etc.)	I make friends easily and effortlessly. People like me.
☹ The world is a dangerous place and you just cannot trust people.	People will hurt me or try to take advantage of me if given the chance. I don't feel safe. I need to protect myself.
☺ Life is an endless opportunity for learning and growth.	When I seek I find. All my life experiences are shaping my understanding and development.

It takes awareness to identify, and a firm decision to change those (negative) core beliefs that *do not* serve you.

Let's identify the core beliefs that underpin *your* life, influence your self-belief, your thinking, and your decisions. Remember that the story that you've been telling yourself has been influenced by others when you were growing up. You *can* decide to change it.

Negative **Core Beliefs**☹	**Associated Thoughts** **You can decide NOW to CHANGE to more empowering thoughts** Toss out the associated thought that was wrong and does not serve you!
I am weak	*Decide to throw out the old belief and embrace the truth instead:* The truth is that I am strong in many ways: my resolve, my physical power, my morals, The truth is that I find ways to develop my strength daily.
I am a failure	*Decide to throw out the old belief and embrace the truth instead:* The truth is that I succeed in many ways: I am a good friend, father/ mother/ sister/ brother/ worker/ etc. The truth is that I find ways to experience small successes daily and I build on this.
I will always be overweight	*Decide to throw out the old belief and embrace the truth instead:* The truth is that I love and care for myself and want to be healthy and energetic. To reach my optimum weight I am focussing on my goal and commit to taking daily action. I take action by formulating a good plan for a healthy diet and daily exercise and make these my habits! I take action by eliminating 'non-foods' from my life, ie. sugar, refined foods, excessive simple carbohydrates, soft drinks, fried food, etc.
I never win	*Decide to throw out the old belief and embrace the truth instead:* I win whenever I set a goal and take action to achieve it. I achieve goals that I really want to achieve when I put my mind to it. I win when I become clear on my goal/mission, focus on it, and take action. I take action by formulating a good, step-by-step plan and put one foot in front of the other!

I am not good enough	*Decide to throw out the old beliefs and embrace the truth instead:*
	There is no such thing as the perfect person!! Each person is different and each of us are 'enough'!
	These are some amazing things about me:
	I am strong, I am principled, I am honest,
	I am hard-working, I am trustworthy, I am loyal,
	I am funny, I am unique, I am kind...
	... (think of ALL the truths about how good you are! and write them here. Keep these thoughts in your mind!) Write them on a poster that you keep on your wall – and look at every day – if you need reminding!
I often feel angry.	*Decide to throw out the old belief and embrace the truth instead:*
	It is OK to feel anger in an appropriate way.
	I understand that everyone has a different perspective, and that they are all doing the best they can with the resources that they have. I merely need to discuss any issues we may have and find a solution.
	I focus on gratitude and positivity. I see the upside of every situation. I breathe, and connect to the calm within ...
I feel sorry for myself ... nothing ever goes right in my life.	*Decide to throw out the old belief and embrace the truth instead:*
	The truth is that I experience small successes every day.
	I choose to focus on what goes right and I notice more and more that things *do* go right and when I look for those successes I see more and more of them daily.
	There is no reason to feel sorry for myself because I now have proof that things do go right.
I find it difficult to open up and make friends.	*Decide to throw out the old belief and embrace the truth instead:*
	I can relax and just be myself.
	I know that I am a worthwhile person with a good heart.
	I am a good friend who is worth knowing.

I always get rejected.	*Decide to throw out the old belief and embrace the truth instead:* I realise that I am the only person who determines how I feel and the only approval that I need is my own. *I think you are getting the idea of how you can change these mistaken beliefs to better fit reality of who you are and your unique magnificence and to bring this to your consciousness instead of the erroneous garbage that you may have been operating with, in the past.*
My opinion doesn't matter.	*Decide to throw out the old belief and embrace the truth instead:* My opinion is as valid as any else's opinion. I am worthwhile. I am valid. I matter. I am love. I am kindness. I am ……
People are selfish, self-serving, and untrustworthy.	*Decide to throw out the old belief and embrace the truth instead:* This is a story and not the truth: I choose to see the good in others.
…	Your turn to add your own specific negative beliefs. Ask yourself: in the past, what have been the feelings that I wanted to avoid having to feel?
I am …	…
Life is …	…
People …	…
…	…

Let's also identify and support your (positive) core beliefs that *do* serve you!

If you foster this positive self-talk and empowering beliefs and have those thoughts underpinning your life, your thinking, and your experience of life, will change completely.

DONNA PORTLAND

☺ Positive **Core Beliefs**	**Associated thoughts**
I believe in myself.	My choices are entirely up to me. My choices are completely valid.
I am friendly and genuine.	I relate well to others. I make friends easily.
I love my body.	I take care of my body: nourish it and keep fit.
I put my best efforts into everything that I do.	I invest myself into what I do. If I fail, I learn from it in order to succeed in the future.
I am worthwhile.	I am the only person who determines how I feel. I approve of myself 100%.
I am grateful for everything that I am and that I have.	Life is a wonderful gift that I am making the most of every day.
I am positive about life.	I can see the upside and believe that there is a gift of learning in everything that happens.
	Now your turn to add your own.
...	

"Your personal core values
define who you are.
Character is destiny."

Tony Hsieh [34], American internet entrepreneur
and venture capitalist.

---

[34] Tony Hsieh transformed Zappos (online shoe store) with these five core values: delivering exceptional service, driving change and expansion, create a strong culture, communicate in an open way, and always improve yourself!

DONNA PORTLAND

Concerning your values:

Are they serving you?
How can you change them?

Returning to the idea of values; we all have values that govern all aspects of our lives. The truth is that you will experience greater fulfillment when you live by your values. Have you ever noticed that your physical state suffers when you don't honour your values? This was abundantly true in my life. I valued health and vitality but had slumped into bad habits of sitting around watching TV instead of being active. I ate too much of the wrong foods (biscuits, pate, dips, chips, chocolate, ice cream, and so on) I knew that I was experiencing dissonance with my values versus my behaviour, but I ignored it, and that didn't work. I was only able to feel centred and fulfilled when I owned the truth - that I had let my standards drop, decided to change my habits and chose to consistently honour my values.

Our values highlight what we stand for and represent our unique essence. Our values are our code of conduct and guide our behaviour. When we are incongruent with our values this is when we allow bad habits to dominate and we can experience regression into childish (often narcissistic) behaviours.

What are *your* values? You have already identified your top values relating to three areas of your life that you would like to improve. You can use the list of positive core values below to assist in becoming aware of your values in all spheres of your life. Feel free to add more as this is not an exhaustive list.

Positive Core Values List

Acceptance	Authenticity	Challenge
Accomplishment	Authority	Charity
Accountability	Autonomy	Citizenship
Accuracy	Awareness	Clean
Achievement	Balance	Clear
Adaptability	Beauty	Clever
Adventure	Boldness	Comfort
Affection	Bravery	Common Sense
Alertness	Brilliance	Communicative
Altruism	Calm	Community minded
Ambition	Candour	Compassionate
Amusement	Capability	Competent
Assertiveness	Certainty	Concentration

Confident
Connection
Contribution
Controlled
Convicted
Cooperative
Courageous
Courteous
Creative
Credible
Curious
Decisive
Dedicated
Dependable
Determined
Devoted
Dignified
Disciplined
Discover-ability
Driven
Effective
Efficient
Egalitarian
Empathic
Empowered
Enduring
Energetic
Enjoyment
Enquiring
Enthusiastic
Ethical
Excellent
Experienced
Explorative
Expressive
Fair
Faithful
Family-oriented
Famous
Fearless
Ferocious

Fit
Flexible
Focussed
Foresighted
Fortitudinous
Freedom
Friendships
Full of ideas
Full of Potential
Full of Wonder
Fun
Generosity
Genius
Giving
Goodness
Grace
Gratitude
Greatness
Growth
Happy
Hard working
Harmonious
Having faith
Healthy
High Status
Honest
Honour
Hopeful
Humble
Humourous
Illuminated
Imagination
Improved
Improvised
Independent
Individual
Influential
Ingenious
Innovative
Insightful
Inspiration

Integrity
Intelligent
Intense
Intuitive
Irreverent
Joyful
Just
Kind
Knowledgeable
Lawful
Leader
Learning
Loving
Loyal
Masterful
Mature
Meaningful
Moderate
Moral
Motivated
Of Service
Open
Optimistic
Ordered
Organised
Original
Passionate
Patient
Peaceful
Performer
Persistent
Physically Healthy
Playful
Pleasant
Poised
Popular
Powerful
Present
Productive
Professional
Prosperous

Purposed
Quality
Realistic
Reasonable / Unreasonable
Recognised
Recreational
Reflective
Religious
Reputation
Respectful
Responsible
Restrained
Results-oriented
Reverent
Rigorous
Risk-taking
Satisfactory
Secure
Self-Reliant
Self-Respect
Selfless
Sensible

Sensitive
Serene
Sharing
Significant
Silent
Simple
Sincere
Skilled
Skilful
Smart
Spiritual
Spontaneous
Stable
Stoic
Strong
Structured
Successful
Supportive
Surprising
Talented
Tenacity
Thankful

Thorough
Thoughtful
Timely
Tolerant
Tough
Traditional
Tranquil
Transparent
Trusting
Trustworthy
Truthful
Understanding
Unique
United
Valorous
Victorious
Vital
Warm
Wealthy
Welcoming
Winning
Wise

Negative Core Values List

Anger
Impatience
Judgement

Rejection
Self-pity

... your choice...
... your choice...

When you analyse your core values you will be able to see clearly where you are being inauthentic or living inauthentically. What is *not* serving you?

When you become aware, that's when you can decide to make changes: <u>what</u> you want to change, <u>how</u> you will do it (your plan) and most importantly to <u>take action</u> and start doing it.

However, be aware and EXPECT:

- **Fear** – almost always that fearful little voice will rise up and tell you that what you're doing is a waste of time, will never work, will make a fool out of you, is too hard, and so on. Don't let fear control you. Instead control your fear! Keep doing the ongoing work (learning, meditating, reflecting, growing, gratitude, et al) to maintain control of your mind.

- **Discomfort** – if you want to transform from your old way of doing things be prepared to get out of your comfort zone. This is where maximum growth takes place!

- **Uncertainty** - if you can learn to be ok with not knowing (the outcome, how people will react, what the future holds, what opportunities will present themselves, who you may meet, etc.) you'll be open to possibilities!

- **Indecision/Procrastination/Distraction** – Life gets in the way. Your mind gets in the way. Old habits try to sneak back in. The trick here is to recognise what is happening and **keep re-focussing on your goal or plan**. Sometimes you actively have to push yourself out of your inertia.

Know yourself: go within

Experiment and learn

Keep growing: step outside your comfort zone!

Take responsibility

Express your gratitude

Listen to your intuition

Be prepared

Identify opportunities

Keep your eyes (and your mind) open

Take action on the knowledge you gain

Keep focussed

Recognise when you are being inauthentic: refocus

Tap into your creativity

Embrace faith (conscious redirection of your imagination!)

Fear vs. Faith

What's the difference? Both are made up notions. They are experiences of life and are built out of your imagination. Fear is imagination undirected (worst case scenario) and faith is your power to consciously direct your imagination and create what you want in life. This is powerful. Clearly it is your choice as to which you focus on.

Anthony Robbins expresses it beautifully:

> # "Fear is you imagining the worst.
>
> # Faith is you imagining a higher purpose."

Bringing faith to an uncertain situation is one of the greatest resources you can have. Of course, there are no guarantees in life, but the alternative is to believe that the worst (your fear) will happen or you can focus on a positive result instead. Which mindset do you think works best? Which feels better to adopt?

I want to quote from one of Robbins' blogs, as this perfectly communicates the reason for persevering with an attitude or a mindset of having faith in a positive outcome:

"If you develop that level of faith, you have an advantage in this game. We don't get big muscles from the easy stuff. We become more because we've been through life's difficulties."

No matter what happens, you succeed or fail; either way you have a positive opportunity to learn and grow. Clearly though, if your expectation and beliefs are on the positive side then it is more likely that you will succeed and grow. If you veer towards negativity and fear then you are much more likely to crash and burn!

DON'T PUT THE BOOK DOWN

Now that you are clear about your beliefs and values...

DONNA PORTLAND

The next step is to make a decision about what happens next in your life!

How to make a viable plan to achieve your goal(s).

There is an old saying that goes something along the lines of
"If you fail to plan, then you are planning to fail".
It's true. You need to have an idea of what you are aiming to achieve and then create a viable plan to reach it.

*The greatest predictor
of future results is
shaped by: INTENTION*

INTENTION
+ ENERGY
+ HABITS
= RESULTS

Here are the steps to make viable plans:

Viable plans are known as SMART goals, which are Specific, Measurable, Achievable, Relevant and Time-bound. If you want to develop two or three smart goals to help you focus your efforts over a timeframe; three, six, nine or twelve months, and it is possible to have them happening concurrently.

State your goal

Example: paying off debt*.

> **Specific**: I will pay off $5,000 in debt.

> **Measurable**: I will apply at least $250 each month to that debt.

> **Achievable**: I can achieve this if I cut back on my cable TV, mobile phone plan, cappuccinos and other incidental spending.

> **Relevant/Realistic**: I need to reduce my debt to apply more money to savings and future goals.

> **Timely**: I will pay off this debt in 1 year and 8 months or less.

* Setting financial goals is an important step toward gaining control of your finances.

Example steps:

Specific things I can do to reach my goal When? Do now or 'by...'

Freeze (or cancel) my cable TV subscription.	now
Eat at home more than going out.	now
Drink less alcohol.	now
Think up a list of fun things to do (with friends/family etc.) that don't cost lots of money: i.e. free, cheap, or good value.	Within the week
Set up an auto-debit from my bank account to pay $250 each month to my loan. Add a reminder to my calendar to check the account balance to ensure sufficient funds are available.	now
...	
...	

Now you can fill in *your* goal:

Is it Specific?	
Is it Measurable?	
Is it Achievable?	
Is it Relevant?	
Is it Time-bound?	

Now get clear about the actual steps you will take and when you will take them!

Specific things I can do to reach my goal	**When? Do now or 'by...'**

Now that you have articulated your smart goal, it is up to you to follow through and make it happen. It may help to tell people so that you are bound to follow through!

The greatest predictor of future results is shaped by:
INTENTION + ENERGY + HABITS = RESULTS

When your new positive habits cause you to start achieving small wins it will motivate you towards further wins and start a positive cycle.

POSITIVE HABITS GET RESULTS!

Consider coaching:

A great way of keeping on track and keeping focussed is to have a coach assist you. You may not be aware that most successful people on the planet have had life coaches and continue to receive support from professional consultants! You may not realise that NLP techniques and knowledge is used by many prominent people such as Oprah Winfrey, Tony Robbins, Richard Branson, Bill Gates, and Donald Trump just to name a few ... as well as most CEOs and successful salespeople around the globe. The benefits from coaching is that you will get to where you want to go faster when you have someone to guide and encourage you, plus keep you positively directed and on track.

A coach can specifically help you deal with the negatives in your past, removing blockages that may be preventing you from moving forward, removing limiting beliefs that keep you stuck, and perhaps re-programme (using NLP methods) any thinking that is not serving you.

CHAPTER 18

MEASURE YOUR PROGRESS – STAY ON TRACK

OK, you've done the hard yards. You have identified where you've gotten off track in your life and you've made smart plans to achieve results. Well done! I wish you every success - from the start and ongoing. Yes - ongoing.

It's all very well to lose 20kg but not OK to lose those hard-won new positive habits - the ones you adopted to lose the weight in the first place - by taking your eye off the ball and having that weight sneak back on!

It is essential to stay motivated to keep going, to continue to take those steps each day, to maintain your wins and your new improved existence. Most of the time it doesn't feel like an effort because those new healthy and positive habits will maintain on their own simply because you are continuing to act on them, and it has become second nature. However, it is also possible to stray back to old diehard bad habits. So how do you prevent that from happening?

Keep FOCUSSED:
Don't forget your "*Why?*"

Feed the drive to stay on target: remind yourself whenever you need to, about your original motivation to transform. Go back in your mind to remember how bad that felt - to remind yourself that you have moved on from there! Imagine your utopia instead and how good *that* feels.

Notice your negative triggers. Be mindful of avoiding the places/people/situation etc. that may cause you to go off-track - like a recovering alcoholic would studiously avoid bars and places that they would be tempted to drink.

Tell people that you are doing something. Then you will have to live up to your promise! This is a powerful motivator.

Don't get stuck in your head. We all know how *that* feels don't we? That annoying little voice in the back of your mind (your ego) that doesn't stop piping up to tell you a bunch of drivel that keeps you from taking action. When you get stuck in your head your energy is sapped and your motivation wanes, and you fail to take positive action.

No turning back! Don't give yourself an out if you really want to achieve something. When you have made your plans and strategies, this is the time to stay focussed and keep going: step by step. It is too easy to hit snooze on the alarm clock, turn over and go back to sleep, but by skipping out on your gym session you are only letting yourself down. So, hold yourself to a higher standard and keep your word - to yourself. I found that if I had prepared everything the night before, and no thinking was required the next day, I could just get up, pull on the clothes, grab the bag and head out the door at 5:30am.

Don't get stuck in a time zone (past, present, or future). Life is lived NOW, so if you catch yourself living other than now, it's time to re-focus and get back to being present in the moment.

Use your physiology to change state.

Remember that:

ZERO ENERGY = ZERO MOTIVATION

That means when you need a "rev up" you can pull out one of these clever tactics to get the energy back:

- Five quick-succession deep breaths. Repeat if necessary.
- Go for a brisk walk.
- Crank up the volume on some funky music.
- Dance to an upbeat song.
- Start laughing and roll around on the floor.
- Sing loudly – preferably an upbeat song.
- "30-30-30" With your feet planted firmly on the floor (one foot in front of the other like you're about to start a running race) bend forward by 30^0 from the hip and start pumping your arms back and forward like you're running. Do this fast for 30 seconds. If you need more, then do another 30.

I guess which one(s) you pick depends on where you are at the time you need to do it - otherwise you might raise a few eyebrows! But do you care ...?

Measure your progress by keeping records, charts, collecting facts, and asking questions to yourself about your progress. This is proof to yourself and others that your positive habits are making the difference that you wanted. Journals are great for this.

EPILOGUE

*Life is a gift
and we owe it
to ourselves
to live it well.*

The title of this book is so because of the evident truth that Positive Habits Get Results. That was my experience, and still is. I had some destructive and useless habits that were ultimately causing me pain and misery. When I became conscious of where I was, I could decide to make changes. When I regained my energy, I found the motivation to continue the journey towards living my best life. This is true for you too.

Congratulations for getting to the epilogue and I hope that you enjoyed and learned from the journey through 18 chapters!

Over the period of time that it's taken to compile all my learnings and discoveries, some twelve months or so, there has been an enormous amount that life has thrown at me to divert me from my goals: I got divorced – I moved house (twice) – I broke my arm – I got quite sick with the 'flu (pre Coronavirus!!) – my assistant resigned to go travelling – I moved offices (twice) – my elder sister died – my family's property on the south coast was burned by the summer fires (2019/2020) – my brother-in-law died – the Coronavirus Pandemic happened, lockdown etc. etc. I could have used all this as an excuse for not finishing or giving up, but I decided to refocus each time and get back to basics.

I broke my arm when I momentarily lost focus and the repercussions were huge! I had to find the lesson in that and learn to keep my eye on the ball. The kilos crept back on when my injury meant that I couldn't get to the gym and the old (bad habit) lethargy returned. I had to first recognise what had happened and refocus on getting back on track. Whenever I diverted from the good habits I had adopted I felt a decline in motivation and a return to old ways. When I forgot to meditate I lost focus. I think you get the picture.

The moral of that story is that we each deserve to be living our best life every day - not in fits and starts - but ongoing. It is our daily habits that show us who we are. You can tell just by looking at someone whether they take time for themselves: to keep their body healthy and their mind inspired. Without health and vitality, you are running on empty and you're not living your best life.

I hope that this compilation of ideas, research and insights will help you to tune up your life where you need it and wish you well in getting the most enjoyment from your life that's possible.

Namaste.

Donna

PS

Contact me if you would like personal coaching. There is an application process however, as I will only work with people who are ready to take action to change their lives NOW.

- My website is DonnaPortland.com
- Join the mailing list to be notified of events and offerings in the future.
- Stay tuned for online courses in the near future.
- Stay tuned for retreat weekends.
- Feel free to LIKE my Donna Portland Facebook page.

Again, I wish you well.

Donna

Printed in the United States
By Bookmasters